FAITH
The Key
to Success

FAITH
The Key
to Success

Henry Fernandez

Evergreen
PRESS

Faith: The Key to Success
by Henry Fernandez

ISBN 1-58169-065-7
For worldwide distribution.
Printed in the U.S.A.

Evergreen Press
P.O. Box 91011 • Mobile, AL 36691
800-367-8203

Table of Contents

Special Thanks

To Carole, my wife and princess

In honor of your love, concern, care,
and inspiration that encourages me to reach my goal
and make the right decisions at all times.
I appreciate you!

Thank you for being there as a tower of strength
to remind me that I can't quit serving God
because He is the one who called me
and He's able to see me through any and every turmoil
or volcano that erupts in my life.

Thanks for your motivation, dedication
and untiring effort for every step you take beside me.
With love...

Dedication

To Seion-Zane, my first-born miracle son

You are truly far more precious than gold.
After five, ten, fifteen years of marriage
(the waiting seemed like forever),
the Lord gave you to us.
Seion, your conception and birth have truly
inspired and motivated my faith in God even more.
I kept trusting Him even when it seemed like
maybe you would be conceived
after 20 years of marriage.

Son, in honor of my love and dedication to provide for
you and to be a living example for you to follow,
I dedicate my second book to you.
My faith in God increased while trusting Him
for you and this opened another horizon
of my faith in God.
I love you dearly.

Acknowledgments

To Dr. (Bishop) Isaiah Campbell
(my former pastor)

Thank you for believing and recognizing the call of God on my life ten years ago. Your trust, confidence, and blessing upon me to go forth and answer the call of God ten years ago has truly proven to be worthwhile. Not many leaders believe in encouraging others to possess the land and preach the gospel, but you were definitely born to change the world by stimulating the ability in others to produce great success in the kingdom of God.

To Michael Chitwood
(Chitwood Accounting firm)

Your inspiration, knowledge, honesty and boldness have truly changed my outlook on the ministry. You helped me to realize that God's business must be in order. I've really come to understand that not just in the pulpit, but in every accounting transaction in the ministry, professionalism and accountability is the key to maintaining a ministry of integrity. Thank you! You've helped to increase my faith by your wise counsel.

Introduction

Faith is not a trait that comes naturally to us humans. When I think about Peter walking on the water to Jesus, I have a feeling that most of us would have stumbled just as Peter did. Even though he was privileged to see all the miracles that Jesus had done, he still had a problem with completely putting his faith in God.

The more we learn and understand God's Word, the more we can walk in faith in our everyday life. Writing this book has reminded me of the many times in my life when faith has made the difference between success and failure.

Today, many people long to achieve success—financial prosperity, exceptional health, meaningful relationships, and more—only to have their hopes dashed to the ground. Even Christians can become discouraged and disappointed when their dreams go unfulfilled.

They pray. They believe, they believe, they believe—but nothing happens. Has God turned a deaf ear? Is their faith in vain? They even wonder if they should spend their time and spiritual energies pursuing personal success and a better life for their families. If you don't know the Word of God, these issues will confuse you.

But if you understand and are assured of the promises of God, and have the key to unlock those promises for your own life, blessings will overtake you. What is the key? Faith, of course. But faith is so misunderstood today.

Some people think faith is a magic bullet that will help you to get what you want from God. But faith can't be reduced to a seven or even a twelve step formula. Strong faith—the kind that releases the blessings of God—only comes when we hear, believe and act on the promises God has made to us in the Scriptures.

When God speaks a Word into your life and you trust Him for it and believe in it, that Word is going to work for you. It is a sure Word. You don't need to copy anyone else's success. You can look at their success and encourage yourself. But you will be able to complete the vision God has put into you because your faith is in His Word!

It's time for us to begin to act as successful people, people of destiny. It's time for us to believe in ourselves, to believe that we are full of potential, and our present situation is only a stepping stone to where we are going. Your environment may look different than what you are saying in faith, but that is how faith works. You don't have to see it to believe it and declare it.

When my wife and I were childless for so long, every Father's Day I said, "One day..." and then that day finally came. Some of you need to drive through some neighborhoods and say, "One day...." Some of you need to drive by some businesses and say, "One day...." If you are waiting for a healing, say, "One day...." If you are waiting for a wife, say, "One day...."

There are things in this life that God wants you to birth. No one else on the earth can birth them but you. But you must be sensitive to His timing. You may wonder how long your struggles will last. The answer from God is that passion plus timing equals success.

It's time to do something you have never done before. step out of the norm. Get away from your comfort zone. Start taking risks. Believe that God wants to bless you and take the risk. Step out by faith and stand on His Word. If He says you are going to be successful, then go after success. While you go after success, the blessings of the Lord will make you rich.

I pray that the Holy Spirit will open your understanding so that you can have great faith. You can have the blessings of God if you want them. They are available to you. They will not come easy; you have to be persistent. You may even need to be desperate. Do something you have never done before and watch God move in your life today!

Finally, I want you to understand that your love for God shouldn't be based on what you can get from Him. When you're mature, you can go to God and not have to ask Him for a blessing. What you will ask for is a heart to serve Him and worship Him. You won't have to ask Him to pay off your credit cards or make you debt free. You'll be mature enough to realize this will happen when you seek Him first.

I invite you now to open the Word of God and unlock its riches—spiritual, material, emotional, and physical—by using your faith, the key to successful living. And, may God richly bless all that you set your mind, heart, and hands to do!

When God speaks a Word into your life
and you trust Him for it
and believe in it, that Word
is going to work for you. It is a sure Word.
You don't need to copy anyone
else's success. You can look at their success
and encourage yourself.
But you will be able to complete the vision
God has put into you
because *your faith is in*
His Word!

Faith Is an *Action* Word

And Jesus answering saith unto them, Have faith in God.

For verily I say unto you, That whosoever shall say unto this mountain, Be thou removed, and be thou cast into the sea; and shall not doubt in his heart, but shall believe that those things which he saith shall come to pass; he shall have whatsoever he saith.

Therefore I say unto you, What things soever ye desire when ye pray, believe that ye receive them, and ye shall have them.(Mark 11:22-24)

Basketball players have it. Astronauts have it too. Entrepreneurs, musicians, scientists, architects, and Christians all have it. What is it? *Faith!* They all have faith in the people who made their machines or instruments, faith in their own ability or creativity, and some even have faith in God. Faith is what makes their life exciting and new discoveries, compositions, designs, and inventions possible. When Christians meet life head on with faith, *challenges become opportunities*. Faith is the key that unlocks the unexpected treasures that are hidden among the problems of everyday life.

Obstacles to a Powerful Faith

Unfortunately some people have robbed themselves of the kind of faith that enables them to face each day with anticipation. Instead, they've treated faith as a dry, boring subject that is taken out on Sunday mornings, dusted off, looked at for a moment, and then put away for the rest of the week.

Other people try to force their faith into a formula with seven principles or twelve easy steps. But faith is too big a concept to be taught in steps and principles. It must be taught as powerfully and simply as it appears in the Word of God with both the lessons and the miracles that are recorded on page after page. Faith is *believing* what the Word of God says and *acting* on it. In fact, the Bible tells us faith without works is dead (Jas. 2:20). If every one of us would apply the Word of God to our situation, God in His own way would work powerfully in it for His honor and for His glory—and *our lives would never be the same again!*

Another reason why people don't walk in powerful faith is because they think faith can be developed by *hearing someone's testimony.* Romans 10:17 says that "Faith cometh by hearing, and hearing by the Word of God." These people would change the verse to read: Faith cometh by hearing and hearing by my neighbor's testimony. You can see how ridiculous that sounds. A person's testimony should only be used to *encourage you or affirm what you already believe.*

We shouldn't base our faith on someone else's experience. Each one of us is unique, and our walk of faith in God will be just as unique...and exciting. Each of us must get into the Word for ourselves and have *our own experiences with God*. When you hear a brother or sister share a testimony of how God did something on their behalf, rejoice and use that testimony to encourage yourself to believe God for *your* circumstances, no matter how difficult they seem to be.

One of the things we need to understand is that God operates in many different ways. His ways are not our ways, and His thoughts are not our thoughts (Is. 55:8).

He created us totally different from each other. Therefore when we read His Word, we cannot try to make it operate a certain way *all the time* for every one of us.

Faith In Your Own Gifts

Today, many people desire to become successful entrepreneurs. Because of their burning passion to pursue their dream, they read magazines and books about successful businesspeople. They see how much faith and total confidence these people have in their God-given abilities. Unfortunately, it is at this point that people make the mistake of getting confidence from other peoples' testimony, by saying, "Hey, if he did it, so can I!" In other words, they have faith in the experiences of others and not in their own God-given gifts. They don't get into His Word and see what God says to them about their situation. And so when they come up against the inevitable problems, they give up and judge themselves to be failures.

The Bible declares that God knew you even before the foundation of the world. He knew where your beginning was going to be, and He knows where your ending is going to be. Since God's Word is true, you know that everything you are ever going to become is already completed. He says to you, "I have seen what you will accomplish; now you just have to believe me to walk you through the process."

What do you believe now? Do you believe you have the ability to succeed now? If you believe this, you are already on the path to success!

A Heart Confession

If you can believe, I mean *really believe* in God and what He can do through your life, you *will see* the manifestation of what you believe. Proverbs 23:7 says, "As a man thinketh in his heart, so is he." *Believing has to do with the heart.* After you believe and confess through your mouth what God has said, without a doubt, you will receive what He has promised you.

This process is similar to what happens with salvation. If you believe in your heart and confess with your mouth the Lord Jesus Christ, then you shall be saved. The word "saved" has to do with deliverance. You shall be delivered from your sins. You will receive the Savior, the Lord Jesus Christ into your life. That is what believing does. You believe, you confess it, and you are saved.

Christians today say things they don't even believe. They *claim* many times over that they believe, but in their heart they do not have a firm belief in the abundant promises of God for them. The Bible tells us that "Abraham staggered not at the promise of God" (Rom. 4:20). He believed God; he continued steadfast in his faith. That is what we must do. If we don't waver in our belief in God, then we will progress more swiftly down the path of success.

In corporate America, there are many people who are loaded with potential. But they cannot use their potential to become successful because they really do not believe they have what it takes to make it. They may have the ability to do many things, but they accomplish nothing because of fear and doubt. Therefore, they will never succeed. For a Christian, having faith means you actually know in your heart and have full assurance that God will bring it to pass.

It is my prayer today that you would not just confess what you believe, but your confession would be a *heart confession*. That is how success is going to come to you. You have to believe it in your heart. You have to feed on it and meditate on it day and night. If you believe it, you will begin to confess it, regardless of what you see around you.

Success Is Just a Few Yards Away

I would like to share with you my personal testimony of how God called me to become a pastor. Becoming a pastor was the last thing I wanted. There were other things on my agenda. Finally after searching the Word and much prayer, I started believing that God ordained for me to become a successful pastor.

The moment I took up the challenge and believed it in my heart, I went forth and did what God told me to do. I put all of my energy and my effort into it. I confessed it day and night, not just mentally, but in my heart. I confessed it *from* my heart, *through* my lips. I declared things that the circumstances around me did not seem to warrant. It did not look like I was going to be successful. But what I have found is that *once you make up your mind to believe in something, success is just a few yards away.*

I remember when we began holding services in an elementary school and called it The Faith Center. At these services, I preached to my wife alone. I thought to myself, *My God, what did I get myself into?* You need to understand that I came from a church that usually had about 600 in attendance every Sunday, so for us to meet by ourselves was a leap of faith. We had been in a comfortable environment, but now God called us away for a new challenge. He said, "I put the gift of pastoring in you, now I want you to go forward and accomplish it. I have finished the work in you already. All I need you to do is be obedient and believe me."

I want you to know just how difficult it was to start that church and watch my wife sitting alone in the "audience." Sometimes I was tempted to think I was crazy and had missed God. But I believed in myself and what He had told me. I believed that He who began a good work in me was able to perform it until the day of Jesus Christ (Phil. 1:6).

I was able to accomplish what God wanted me to do because of my firm belief in His promises to me. The Faith Center is now a congregation of over 5,000 people with three services on Sundays because one man decided in his heart that he was going to believe what God said to him.

Now I'm not going to tell you that if you take my testimony and believe it, everything will happen in the same way for you. Remember, we are all unique, and God deals individually with each of us. Maybe God has not called you to be a pastor, or maybe He has called you to be the pastor of a church with a different vision. What worked for me may not work in the same way for you because we may not be called to do the same work. Faith works in whatever way God wants it to...but it definitely works. He said His Word will not return to Him void. *It will always accomplish what He sent it to do.*

Faith Deals With the Present

Some Christians don't *believe* what the Word of God says—they just *hope* that its promises will be fulfilled for them. There is a vast difference between faith and hope. Hope has to do with expecting something in the *future*. Faith deals with the *present*. In fact, Hebrews 11:1 says: "Now faith is the **substance** of things hoped for, the evidence of things not seen." Faith is acting on the Word of God when you hear it. Faith is in the present tense. You've got to believe the Word of God *now*.

When God speaks a Word into your life and you trust Him for it and believe in it, that Word is going to work for you. It is a sure Word. You don't need to copy anyone else's success. You can look at their success and encourage yourself. But you will be able to complete the vision God has put into you because *your faith is in His Word*!

It's time for us to begin to act as
successful people,
people of destiny. It's time for us
to believe in ourselves,
to believe that we are full of potential,
and our present situation is only a stepping
stone to where we are going.
Your environment may look different than
what you are saying,
but that is how faith works.
*You do not have to see it to believe it
and declare it.*

Speak to the Mountain

For verily I say unto you, That whosoever shall say unto this mountain, Be thou removed, and be thou cast into the sea; and shall not doubt in his heart, but shall believe that those things which he saith shall come to pass; he shall have whatsoever he saith. (Mark 11:23)

Faith works for everyone regardless of what color they are, regardless of what nationality they are, or whatever culture they come from. Faith works for all people, everywhere, for all time.

Notice in the verse above that Jesus used the word "whosoever" when He was declaring who could powerfully see faith at work in their lives. If you can identify with *whosoever,* faith will work for you.

To make this more personal, I want you to insert your name in place of the word "whosoever." For verily I say unto you, _____ , if you, _____ , shall say unto this mountain, Be thou removed, and be thou cast into the sea; and shall not doubt in your heart, but shall believe that those things which you saith shall come to pass; you shall have whatsoever you saith.

Getting Rid of the Obstacles

The first step you must take toward achieving success is to speak to the mountain. What is the mountain? *The mountain represents whatever obstacle is blocking your vision, blessing, or promise from happening in your life.* If you—whosoever—believe the Word of God, then the Bible says you must command the mountain in your life to move. *You can speak to whatever is blocking you from experiencing all of God's blessings and move it out of the way!*

The mistake many people have made is that instead

of speaking to the mountain, they speak to the blessings, to the gifts, and to the success they desire to have. If God has already told you it is yours, then you don't need to address it. For example, suppose I say to you that I am going to give you a car. Then I drive the car into your driveway and hand you the keys. Now you would be crazy to take the keys and say, "I sure hope I can drive something like this. It's a wonderful car. I hope the car will be mine. I just really want to drive that car one day." That would be a ridiculous thing to do because I have already said that the car is yours to keep.

No, as soon as I turn the keys over to you, you would immediately begin to deal with every obstacle that stands between you and your driving the car. One of the first obstacles is your front door. You are inside your house so you have to open the door to get to your car. Obstacle number two might be your driver's license. You will have to take care of any problems with your driver's license if you want to legally drive the car. Obstacle number three could be insurance. I gave you the car, but I said nothing about insurance. Before you get excited about driving the car, you have to get insurance on the car. All of these potential obstacles really need to be dealt with in order to get you ready to receive your blessing.

Another example might be your business. Maybe you need to deal with your employees. Do you have employees who have caught the vision of the company and want to grow with it? Do they have your best interests at heart? If they don't, you can speak every day about how you want your company to be successful, but the employee who has not caught your vision may be a hindrance to your success and probably has to be dealt with before your business can grow.

If you want to buy a new home, you have to deal with some practical issues. You can't just go into a neighborhood and say, "This is the house I want" and move in that day. Nor do you drive up and begin to speak to the house, "This is my house. I claim it. I know it is mine. I can feel it." No, you don't do that either because that is not going to help you get the house.

The first thing you may really need to do in order to purchase a home is to check your credit; if it is bad, you will need to take steps to repair it. Next, you begin to address the down payment issue by putting money into your bank account. These are some of the practical steps that you need to take. If debt or bad credit are your mountains, you must "speak" to those mountains in order to remove them and fulfill your dream.

Even in relationships, whether you are dating or married, you cannot just talk about wanting to have a good marriage or a good relationship that leads to marriage. You must speak to the obstacles that stand in the way. Those obstacles could be selfishness on your part that keeps you from meeting your partner's needs, the necessity to obtain a job that gives you sufficient income to support a family, or learning how to share your innermost thoughts with each other in order to develop a solid relationship. You'll have to take care of these kinds of obstacles before you can experience success in marriage.

Once you believe in your heart what God has said about your dream, it doesn't take much to speak to the obstacles that stand in your way. You won't let anything block you from going where you are destined to go and doing what you are destined to do because you believe that God has said you will be successful. Therefore, you are willing to take on the challenges before you and destroy every obstacle that comes between you and your dream.

Don't make the mistake of addressing your blessing— it's already there waiting for you. It's already yours. Success is already there. You can get it if you first *address the obstacles* that prevent you from receiving it.

Getting Rid of Doubt

In order to effectively speak to the obstacles in your life, you must get rid of doubt.

For verily I say unto you, That whosoever shall say unto this mountain, Be thou removed, and be thou cast into the sea; and shall not doubt in his heart, but shall believe that those things which he saith shall come to pass; he shall have whatsoever he saith.

Notice what it says in the verse above, "...and shall not doubt in his heart." If you do not believe what God has said, your lack of self-confidence will short-circuit the power you need to deal with the "mountains." You will back down from attempting to remove them from your life and not get anywhere or accomplish anything.

Many people can't face the difficult issues in their life because they don't think they have the power to conquer them. Mental obstacles caused by self-doubt are the most difficult to overcome. When you don't believe what God has said and in your ability to carry it out, your inner man is engulfed in doubt. It is as though there were scales over your eyes. If you can't see yourself as God sees you, you will go to your grave "fully loaded" with unused potential. You *can* experience success in life, so don't be willing to settle for defeat.

Fighting the mental battle is not easy, especially in the beginning. It is far easier to *think defeat* than to actually *live victoriously* by taking on the challenges of life. But it's not enough to sit in your easy chair hoping something good will happen. You have to believe in yourself *now*. You have to work towards it now by removing the doubts and fears through faith in God and His abundant promises to you!

Words Frame Your World

When you believe what God has promised you in His Word, you first *say it before you can begin to act ac-*

cording to it. Your words will actually "frame" your world in a new way. If you correctly frame your world with positive words, your environment will begin to change. Obstacles will be easier to identify and remove, and self-doubt will be banished. You can create a successful world out of your words. That's exactly what God did in creation. In Genesis 1, it says "In the beginning God created the heavens and the earth," and then it goes on to say, "God said let there be...." Everything He spoke came into being.

In the New Testament, He gave us that same power. In John 14:12 its says that we would do even greater works than He did. If that is true, then everything we say, if it is spoken with confidence and based on the Word of God, will become reality. We can begin to make changes in our life with our words.

Negative Words Are Destructive

When people speak doubt, they walk in doubt. Nothing positive happens for them. They are faithful to their doubt. Before you know it, they lose the ability to be successful because they surround themselves with doubt. *Doubt does not attract success; doubt attracts failure.*

If you speak negatively about your marriage, saying that you and your spouse do not love each other any more, then your relationship is never going to be strengthened. If you tell your children they are dumb, worthless, and an embarrassment to the family, you are actually framing their world for failure. If you tell yourself you are broke and will never have any money, you are framing your world with negative words. Yes, it might be true you are broke today. But the faith-key is: Do you believe that your present situation is *permanent* or only a *temporary* state?

Tell yourself, "I should be the head and not the tail (Deut. 28:13); I should be a lender and not a borrower." Begin to speak words about opening a business, if that is what God has spoken to you. Of course you must understand that you are going to have to start small, but until you begin to speak positively about it, you will never be a successful businessperson.

When Brian Keith Williams spoke at my church two years ago, he said, "You are somewhere in the future, and you look much better than you look right now." I constantly tell myself that. You need to repeat that to yourself too: You are somewhere in the future and you look much better than you look right now. God loves you in your present state, but He has a vision of you in the future!

It is time for us to begin to act as successful people, people of destiny. It is time for us to believe in ourselves, to believe that we are full of potential, and our present situation is only a stepping stone to where we are going. Your environment may look different than what you are saying, but that is how faith works. *You do not have to see it to believe it and declare it.* As long as you *know it* and you *believe it in your heart*, it is so. The Bible tells us that we do not walk by sight, we walk by faith (2 Cor. 5:7). We walk by total confidence and trust in the Word of God.

Attitude Determines Altitude

In order to speak words of faith, you must first deal with your attitude. Your attitude always determines your "altitude" or how far you will go in life. If your attitude says, "Well, it is not going to work for me; I am not going to listen to what this person is saying; I am just going to try to work it out for myself..." then you will have placed a limit on the amount of success you will have. If you get turned off by other peoples' success and become jealous and envious, again your attitude will limit who you will become.

There is enough wealth for every single human being on this planet. There is no need for anybody to be left behind with their dreams unfulfilled. If you believe in the abilities God has given you from before the foundation of the earth, and go forth and use them, you will become successful. People are not tapping into their potential because of their attitude. For me, personally, I had to take on a different attitude in order to change my circumstances. The moment I did, success came into my life.

I've seen that happen time and time again with people I have counselled. One day, I had a counselling session with a woman who told me she wanted to start a clothing business. She recognized her talent but didn't really believe she could be successful. Fear came over her every time she tried to open the business. She had friends in the same business, some of whom were very successful. She was afraid they would jealously try to prevent her success so she never shared her ideas with them. Her attitude stemmed from her low self-esteem. She doubted that anyone wanted her to succeed, so she trusted no one and had just about given up the dream of owning her own business.

My counsel to the woman was, "Your attitude needs to change. You have to understand that your business has nothing to do with your friends. What they may do or say about you has no bearing on the success of your business." I encouraged her to change her thinking and believe in herself. I encouraged her to start putting all her energy into developing the business and not into worrying about the actions of her friends. Worrying about what others may think or do can easily paralyze you. This attitude can keep you from fulfilling your dream.

This woman listened to my counsel and now has a wonderfully successful women's clothing boutique in a very sophisticated neighborhood. She is doing quite well—all because her attitude changed.

Perhaps right now you are thinking you cannot do certain things in life because of what people have said or might say about you. If so, you need to change your attitude and begin to think success. Success is like food. No matter where you are in a room, if the food is cooked well, the wonderful aroma will get to your nostrils and cause you to desire to taste it. Because you want to taste it, you will go after it. *The minute you begin to go after it is when you become successful.*

Faith is activated when we know
the Word of God.
We need to hear it over and over again
at church, and we need to read it
again and again in our Bible.
It takes time for us to understand exactly
what God is saying to us.
But God will say it over and over
until we get it!

Activating the Word

So then faith cometh by hearing, and hearing by the Word of God (Romans 10:17).

Many Christians have been attending church for a long time, but if you were to ask them if Christianity is making a difference in their lives, what would they say? A large number would probably have to admit that they are not experiencing significant growth or victory.

What is wrong? Obviously there is nothing wrong with the power in the Word and nothing wrong with the power of their salvation. What then is the problem?

For Moses describeth the righteousness which is the law, That the man which doeth those things shall live by them.

But the righteousness which is of faith speaketh on this wise, Say not in thine heart, Who shall ascend into heaven? (that is, to bring Christ down from above:)

Or, Who shall descend into the deep? (that is, to bring up Christ again from the dead.)

But what saith it? The Word is nigh thee, even in thy mouth, and in thy heart: that is, the Word of faith, which we preach.

That if thou shalt confess with thy mouth the Lord Jesus, and shalt believe in thine heart that God hath raised him from the dead, thou shalt be saved. (Romans 10:5-9)

The Word of God gives us a clear understanding of salvation in the verses above. Salvation is not by works. Salvation does not come from the church you are a member of. Salvation is not something that is handed down to you by your ancestors.

The following verses tell us that the way we receive salvation is to *receive* the Word and *believe* it in your heart and then *confess* it with your mouth.

> *For with the heart man believeth unto righteousness, and with the mouth confession is made unto salvation.*
>
> *For the scripture saith, Whosoever believeth on him shall not be ashamed.*
>
> *For there is no difference between the Jew and the Greek: for the same Lord over all is rich unto all that call upon him.* (Romans 10:10-12)

In the same way that salvation is received by the preaching of the Word, so too can we receive a truth or promise from God's Word for us. *We have to believe it and confess it with our mouth and then activate it in our lives.*

The difference between someone who doesn't activate their faith and someone, such as Oral Roberts, who has made faith a priority in their daily walk, is that he understands the way to have strong faith is by hearing the Word. He knows he must spend quality time with God. The Word would never have functioned for him and he would not have been able to build The City of Faith had he not spent quality time in the presence of God.

Spending Quality Time With God

You may ask yourself why the Word isn't functioning for you. Perhaps the reason is because you are not spending quality time with God. Maybe the only time you see and talk with God is once a week, when you show up at church. In today's world it is easy to become busy and not take time to spend a few intimate moments with the Lord. If you don't have intimate moments together in a relationship, after a while you can become separated from one other. To grow in your relationship with Him, you must spend time with Him and His Word.

How then shall they call on him in whom they have not believed? and how shall they believe in him of whom they have not heard? And how shall they hear without a preacher?

How can they hear without a preacher? And how shall they preach, except they be sent? As it is written, How beautiful are the feet of them that preach the gospel of peace, and bring glad tidings of good things! (Rom. 10:14-15)

It is the Word that caused you to first confess Jesus Christ as your Lord and Savior. It is the Word that causes you to believe the report of the Lord. Maybe the reason you don't believe God for all His provision is because *you do not hear the Word enough.*

You have access to all His provision for you by

putting your faith in Him and His Word. But *you must first know what the Word says in order to believe it for your situation.* How can you go to the bank and withdraw funds if you don't know how much money is in your account? You will only go to the bank and withdraw funds if you are sure that you have money there.

For example, in the natural realm, we know we can't take a credit card with $200 available credit and try to buy $400 worth of merchandise. It is the same in the spiritual realm. When we go to God and ask him for a withdrawal, it does not mean our credit is good. It does not mean that just because you ask God for something that He will authorize you to have it. How many people try to get something from God, and He tells them He will not authorize the transaction? You cannot access God's kingdom when you are not accessing the provisions of God in the right way.

Access to God's Provision

Therefore being justified by faith, we have peace with God through our Lord Jesus Christ:

By whom also we have access by faith into this grace wherein we stand, and rejoice in hope of the glory of God.

The Bible tells us in Romans 10:5 to access the provisions of God by *believing in your heart, confessing with your mouth, and following the laws of God.* You will not be able to do it just by coming to church once a week. You must spend time studying the Word of God and letting Him speak to you through it.

When you are tested and the enemy comes against you like a flood, how will you resist him if you are not full of the Word and the Spirit of God? When you slide your Christian "credit card" through the slot, you will not have the credit power to banish him. You will not be able to tell the devil you have spiritual access to God's provision for your health, finances, or your family. You will not be able to say the Lord will fight for you. You will only be able to hold the devil off momentarily while you wait for the Lord to approve your spiritual credit card. Without that spiritual "credit," the Lord will decline your purchase and the devil will stand against you.

Full of the Word

Faith is activated when we know the Word of God. We need to hear it over and over again at church, and we need to read it again and again in our Bible. It takes time for us to understand exactly what God is saying to us. But God will say it over and over until we get it! A good parent will continue to instruct their child until they understand. It takes us time to understand the Word, and so God has to repeat it over and over to us. After time, we begin to see the wonderful provision that He has prepared for us.

We can stand in His provision because it will sustain us for life. That means we are not weak vessels, falling down, and losing ground in God—we are actually gaining ground. The Word of God gives us clear direction to handle the affairs of every area of our life. We can stand in any situation because we understand how faith is activated and know that God makes a way in our lives.

You must be full of the Word in order to function in the way God intended. Many of us think we "know it all" just because we have attended church or Sunday School for so many years. But that is not necessarily true. There may be large parts of the Word that we are ignoring.

For example, sometimes I want to bake something from scratch, so I find a recipe and assemble all of the ingredients. As I start to read the recipe more closely, I may decide I don't want to do all of the necessary steps it lists. Short of time, I may decide to ignore some of the directions so I can quickly get the batter into the oven. Unfortunately these are the times when the end result falls short of what is desired. The reason is because I ignored some of the directions.

I have done the same thing with items that I have bought that must be assembled. I once purchased a computer table that needed to be put together. I started to look at the directions but decided there wasn't time to read them thoroughly, so I just ignored them. When I was done, I felt so proud until I realized I had put the drawer for the keyboard on the wrong side! Can you imagine the trouble I had to go through to take the desk apart and turn the drawer around? When I took the table apart, it lost its stability and was never as strong as it was meant to be.

Some of you may say everything turned out okay because I had a second chance. However, what you fail to realize is that if I had done it right the first time, it would have turned out better. I acted foolishly because I didn't take the time to read the directions.

On another occasion, I went to the store to buy a television set. I got very excited about it because the salesman recognized me and talked about my faith ministry. He demonstrated all of the features of the T.V. for me. It had "picture-in-picture" and a lot of other "bells and whistles." Well, I bought that television, but shortly after I got it home, I realized I should not have done so because I do not have time to use all the T.V.'s benefits.

Do you realize your Bible has many benefits to offer, but you haven't tapped into them yet? You shouldn't say the Christian life is not working for you when you haven't gone to the manual, written by the Maker, and tried to put your life together right in the first place!

*Let us draw near with a **true** heart in full assurance of faith, having our hearts sprinkled from an evil conscience, and our bodies washed with pure water.* (Hebrews 10:22)

You must confess to God if you do not have the Word in you and your faith is not functioning as it should. You must be honest with yourself and know where you are in life. You must know where you are in Christ. Otherwise you will not be able to activate your faith.

The Lord gets really excited when His people live according to His Word and use all the provisions His has for them!

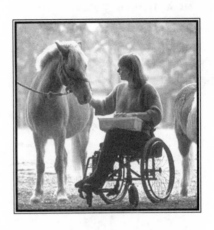

Becoming mature in your faith means
spending time with Him
and activating the Word in your life.
A mature faith is not
where you put in a prayer and
expect to have all your wishes carried out.
God wants us to have a faith
that is used for His purposes—
a holy faith.

Power, Provision, and Promise
Through Patience

My brethren, count it all joy when ye fall into divers temptations;

Knowing this, that the trying of your faith worketh patience.

But let patience have her perfect work, that ye may be perfect and entire, wanting nothing.

If any of you lack wisdom, let him ask of God, that giveth to all men liberally, and upbraideth not; and it shall be given him.

But let him ask in faith, nothing wavering.
(James 1:1-6)

We humans are very impatient by nature. We want the end result of God's provision and power now, but we aren't willing to go through the process to get to it. We bail out quickly because we don't want to deal with temptation.

When we activate the Word of God in our life, we must come to a place where we realize that everything that happens is working patience into us.

God wants us to learn to handle difficult situations properly. It's easy to get angry when things are not going our way. When everything seems upside down at work, we must remember that God is doing something in us. He wants us to change our attitude so He can manifest His glory through us.

What kind of attitude is God looking for in His people? The Apostle says to count it all joy when you experience the trying of your faith because it will work patience in you. *God uses difficult problems to teach you patience.*

We are a nation that loves quick fixes, while God wants us to learn patience. It wasn't so long ago when we didn't have microwaves. People had to get out of bed by 6:00 AM to make breakfast for the entire family. Now each one can get up 30 minutes before it's time for them to leave the house and pop their own breakfast into the microwave. Family members all live in the same house, but they just seem to pass each other coming and going. This "quick fix" style of living is tearing the family apart. When will we see the importance of eating a meal together? Even if we bring home take-out food, we should still sit down and eat together. This forces us to spend time with one another and learn patience with each other.

Learning Contentment

In our impatient rush to get all the "good things in life" we may be hurting our families. Perhaps the reason you are struggling financially is because you are living above your means. Taking on a second job does not really solve the problem because it does not teach you patience. If you are so busy trying to get the "latest and best" you probably don't have enough time to spend with each other.

When you purchase a house, you begin to think about a new sofa, dining room table, and other furniture you would like to have. It's okay to dream, but some of you *think* you are having to bear a heavy burden when you are forced to live with second-hand furniture for a while. If you see these circumstances with the eyes of faith, you will see that God desires to work patience in you.

You can tell whether or not Christians are mature in their faith by how quickly they become upset with each other. One of our ministers said the other day, "Believers should have thick skin." When you are mature, you do not easily get angry over what other people say or leave the church because someone does something bad to you.

If you will allow Him to lead you, He will teach you to appreciate where you are in life. You will have patience with your circumstances and with other people. You will learn to "count it all joy" because your faith is in Him.

Building Yourself Up in the Faith

But ye, beloved, building up yourselves on your most holy faith, praying in the Holy Ghost.

Keep yourselves in the love of God, looking for the mercy of our Lord Jesus Christ unto eternal life. (Jude 1:20-21)

Becoming mature in your faith means spending time with Him and activating the Word in your life. A mature faith is not where you put in a prayer and expect to have all your wishes carried out. God wants us to have a faith that is used for His purposes—a holy faith. This is the kind of faith He wants you to build in your life. But only you can do it. The Bible says you must work out your own salvation. Do not depend on your pastor to do it. Do not depend on a television evangelist to do it. Do not depend on anyone else. You must build yourself up in your most holy faith.

Shield of Faith

Above all, taking the shield of faith, wherewith ye shall be able to quench all the fiery darts of the wicked. (Ephesians 6:16)

If you really want to build yourself up, you must understand that an important aspect of your faith is that you can use it as a shield to keep you from falling into temptation. For example, there are times in your dealings with others when you want to fire back a harsh reply with your mouth, but your faith should tell you to return a soft answer. You may want to give the other person a "piece of your mind," but a soft answer should be your reply. When many women are upset, they tend to shut down—they refuse to cook, clean, or do anything in the house and try to avoid any intimacy that would normally occur. The reason they shut down is because they are not using the shield of faith against what the devil is trying to do in their marriage.

When you build yourself up in the most holy faith, you must realize you are setting yourself up for attack from the enemy. He wants to test you to see how much of the Word you really have inside you. When you put on the shield of faith and the enemy fires darts at you, your faith will shield you. It is impossible for the enemy to penetrate the Word.

Many times we try to confront the enemy with frustration spewing from our mouths. What makes you think you can tell the devil off with that attitude? You need to speak according to the Word. For example, if the devil comes up to you, you will need to be able to say, "I bind you in the name of Jesus." Remember I said to you that the only way we can use a credit card is if we have enough on the card to get an approval? The devil is trying to check out your card. He wants to see if your faith is strong. Many times he will expose the fact that it's not.

When the devil confronts you, you should be able to say, "In whose name are you coming, because you are not coming in the name of Jesus." The moment you say that name in power, the devil has to retreat.

Your flesh can get in the way of walking by faith. When the enemy shoots his fiery darts at you, it is the flesh that wants to come out first, and that is no match for the devil. But when faith is there and the shield covers you, you understand your responsibilities as men and women. You will know the devil is trying to get you out of the divine order. The devil may be trying to get you to dishonor your husband or to say things God would never want you to say to your wife or children.

The Bible says husbands should love their wives as Christ loved the church and gave Himself for it. God expects us to love our wives. He holds them in high honor, even using them to explain his love relationship to the church. The same thing is true for husbands. He wants wives to honor them. And he gave children the commandment to love and respect their parents so it will go well with them and they will prosper.

How many of you would continue reading this book if I asked you to repeat after me, "I deny that Jesus Christ is God; I do not believe He is the Son of the Living God; and I do not believe there is a God anymore?" Many of you would shut this book and probably throw it away. So why do you continually criticize your spouse, which is contrary to God's Word? When you enter your house, you should show love to your husband or your wife. I don't care how imperfect they are. Love them unconditionally and say kind words to them. Don't put them down or ever tell them they are worthless. View them through the eyes of faith and appreciate their true value. *When you build them up in this way you are also building yourself up!*

When my wife and I were childless for so
long, every Father's Day I said,
"One day..." and then that day finally came.
Some of you need to drive
through some neighborhoods
and say, "One day...."
Some of you need to drive by
some businesses and say, "One day...."
If you are waiting for a healing,
say, "One day...." If you are waiting for a wife,
say, "One day...."

If Ye Abide in Me...

If ye abide in me, and my Words abide in you, ye shall ask what ye will, and it shall be done unto you. (John 15:7)

This verse in John contains three important conditions that are essential to understanding how to receive God's blessings. First, "if you abide in me"; second, "if my Words abide in you"; and third, "ye shall ask what you will."

Notice John 15:7 begins with the word "if." In other words, this is a conditional verse. *If you want* the blessings, you *first have to do* something—you have to abide in Him. Jesus revealed to His disciples the unlimited power they have when they abide in Him. He wanted them to understand that the power He possessed to perform the miracles that had impressed them was the same power and authority He would give them if they would abide in Him.

Today, if you abide in Him and His Words abide in you, then *you* have the same authority, the power, and the "password" to ask anything in His name, too. He will give it to you.

God says, "If you abide, you can enter. If you abide in Me, you can have anything you want." When we talk about the word "abide," the Amplified Version puts it this way: "If you *live* in me." The Greek word for abide is *menos* which means to stay in a given place or a state of relation. It means to continue to dwell, to endure, to be present or to stand. In verse seven, Jesus is saying that your blessing will come and you will have the power to stand in every situation if you remain in Him.

The Treasure Chest

Fantasize for a moment about the greatest desires of your heart. What would you have God do for you right now? I am not talking about tomorrow or next year; I am talking about this very moment.

If ye abide in me, and my Words abide in you, ye shall ask what ye will, and it shall be done unto you.

When I read this verse, God showed me His treasure chest and said, "Son, if you want anything you can think of, anything you desire, anything you want—all you have to do is to get the password." God didn't say He would dictate what He is going to give me. I realized that I had to make that decision. God gives us the liberty to pull *anything that we want* out of the treasure chest if we have the password.

The only password that enables you to get your blessing is *faith in God*. I know many people who are trying to get the blessings of God, but they do not want to study His Word or spend time with Him. They want to get it some easier way. They want the preacher to lay hands on them, or they want someone to anoint them with olive oil to release the blessings of God into their life.

Here's an example to more fully explain how a password works. When you turn a computer on, you see it search for the right codes to get it started. Before you can get to the specific screen where you want to work, you are asked for a password that will enable you to enter that restricted area. You may be able to turn the computer on, but you cannot get into the files without a password. If you enter the wrong password, a message says, "Invalid password," and you must enter the correct one. Many of us are trying to get into the treasure chest that holds the blessings and anointing of God. As soon as we put in the correct password, F-A-I-T-H—meaning you have faith in the Word of God and are abiding in it—and you hit the enter key, all the files are available to you.

Now use your imagination again for a moment. Picture the biggest mall you can think of. Then God says to you, "I will wait until the mall closes at 9:00 P.M. and then I will have every store remain open. No one else will be there. All you have to do is show up. I will give you an unlimited opportunity to choose whatever you like." Some people might wander around undecided for hours with such an unlimited choice. In the same way, some of us are waiting for God to tell us what we can have from His treasure chest. But God says, "No—you determine that. All I want you to do is stay in My Word and remain close to Me. Before long, my Word will reveal to you the power and anointing I have poured out upon you and this will enable you to enjoy My provision in your life."

The Power Resides in You

Did you know you have the ability to speak of things your eyes have not seen, your ears have not heard, and your heart has not imagined concerning the things that God has already prepared for you? (1 Co. 2:9). The power is in you, and it is up to you to tap into it. You must only abide. That is all He asks you to do.

You can say you go to church; you can say you are a Christian; but that's not enough. God says not only does He want you to remain in Him, you must also mature, *you must grow.* His Word must take control of you. You are not your own anymore. The anointing of the Holy Spirit has taken over your life. When you do not know what to pray for, the Holy Spirit will lead you.

When the Holy Spirit makes intercession for you, He says things that will blow your mind. There will be times when your flesh tells you that's too much for God to handle. There will be times when your flesh tells you not to talk about what God has promised because people will begin to think you are too ambitious. But you have to re-member that the Holy Spirit is making intercession for you. His Word is in you, and His Word says what God wants you to have.

There are times when your flesh gets discouraged, and it says to you, "Look how long you have been waiting for the promise." When Jesus told his disciples, "If ye abide in Me..." He meant if you live in Me, if you continue in Me, if you stand in Me, if you endure in Me, if you wait in Me and let My Word manifest itself in you, then you will open your mouth and the Holy Spirit will give you boldness. So, if you abide, if you stay in Him, you will meet the first condition. Even in the midst of poverty, you will say to yourself, "I am rich." You may not see it yet, but your time of blessing is coming. *The anointed One says that you are more than a conqueror!*

Your Day Will Come

If you remain in Him, you will be blessed. One day, the house you would like to have will become yours. The enemy will tell you that you will never own it, but God will move on your behalf. If you ask Him for a fish, would He give you a stone? God is not slack concerning His promises. If you open your mouth and declare it, you can believe God for that house and receive it in Jesus' name. Why? Because you abide in His Word and it tells you He will not withhold any good thing from His children (Ps. 84:11).

Your attitude needs to be: "I will not let anyone pour negative ideas into me. I will not let anyone tell me I am not supposed to have God's blessings. I want to enjoy everything that God has for me."

When my wife and I were childless for so long, every Father's Day I said, "One day..." and then that day finally came. Some of you need to drive through some neighborhoods and say, "One day...." Some of you need to drive by some businesses and say, "One day...." If you are waiting for a healing, say, "One day...." If you are waiting for a wife, say, "One day...."

Preparing You for the Blessing

It's "downloading" time. What I sense God doing is downloading things into me. Understand that if you think you should have already gotten some things you have been waiting for, God may be saying, "Not yet." *He may be downloading things into your life to prepare you for your blessing.* I thought I should have already received my children before I did, but God said, "Not yet." I did not have a clue what He was doing. But I waited on Him and told God the only thing missing in my life are the children. But God was downloading things into me and putting some things in order before He could bless us with children.

God may be downloading things into your life right now, but you cannot see it. He may be putting some things in order, but you cannot see it. When your blessing manifests itself, you will say, "What great things He has done!"

From the Beginning

In the beginning was the Word, and the Word was with God' and the Word was God.

The same was in the beginning with God.

All things were made by him; and without him was not any thing made that was made.
(John 1:1-3)

He created anything you and I could ever want in life, from the beginning. There is nothing you could ever dream of that was not already made from the beginning.

You just have to open your mouth and declare those things that are laid up for you. Do not be afraid.

You have been lied to for years. The enemy has told you: "Do not be a dreamer. That's not God's will for you. It's okay to be satisfied where you are. You will never be debt free. You will never purchase a house and pay for it. You will never see your marriage work out. You will never see your kids come to know the Lord Jesus. You will never see your family flourish."

The devil has been lying to you for years, and you have accepted defeat. But Jesus is saying He made all things from the beginning. He knew you would be alive in the 21st century. He knew you would live in the house you have dreamed about. He knew you would drive that car you have long desired. I have better news for you. God knows exactly where you are going to be tomorrow!

Transferring the Power

In him was life; and the life was the light of men. And the light shineth in darkness; and the darkness comprehended it not.

There was a man sent from God, whose name was John.

The same came for a witness, to bear witness of the Light, that all men through him might believe.

He was not that Light, but was sent to bear witness of that Light.

That was the true Light, which lighteth every man that cometh into the world.

He was in the world, and the world was made by him, and the world knew him not.

He came unto his own, and his own received him not.

But as many as received him, to them gave he power to become the sons of God, even to them that believe on his name.

God has revealed Himself to us and has given us power and strength because we belong to Him and are dwelling in Him. As we see this power manifested in our lives and enjoy His blessings, He wants us to pass it along to our children by training them in the Word and in His ways. Now the reason we cannot understand transferred power is because we have not had much to pass along. Instead, we have been transferring only weakness and poverty to the next generation.

When many of us got married, our parents did not provide us with the money to purchase a house or even an example of owning one themselves. They had no wealth to give us and were almost relieved that there was one less mouth to feed. Some of you are so happy that your kids are turning 18 and they can get a job. Why?

Because you are poor. Once you begin to receive the blessings of God and transfer the power to create wealth to your children, it will give you the ability to create even more wealth for God's Kingdom.

Seeing His Glory

Which were born, not of blood, nor of the will of the flesh, nor of the will of man, but of God.

And the Word was made flesh, and dwelt among us, (and we beheld his glory, the glory as of the only begotten of the Father) full of grace and truth. (John 1:13-14)

God wants us to get to the place of blessing where we can see His glory. Do you understand the meaning of glory? Moses said, "Lord show me your glory!"(Ex. 33:13) When God agreed to his request, He could only show him His back. His glory is so awesome that Moses could not see His face and live. God wants us to get to the place where we will not be able to stand because His blessings are so staggering. Everything we touch will be turned around and made into a blessing from Him. It will almost be too awesome for us to handle. Where our lives were once chaos, there will be peace and order. Doors will open to us because of the glory of God.

As you drive down the highway, people will see the glory in you. When you enter your place of work, people will see the glory in you. When others do not understand how you are achieving and receiving such blessings, you can tell them God's glory has touched your life. The glory will be in your face, and the power of God will be upon you. The reason you will succeed when others are struggling will be the power that is working within you. The enemy will not be able to touch you because of the glory.

Speak the glory over your children and your family. Do not allow them to leave for school unless you speak the glory over their lives. God wants us to enjoy the glory. Every Christian should be able to declare that they are living in the glory. If you abide in the Word of God, you will live in the glory.

It is now time to walk in the glory. I don't care what is going on around you. You may be struggling with things in your life, but God says that your struggles are coming to an end. You are going to live in unlimited power as you walk in His truth. God says He is opening up the floodgates of unlimited blessings for you. Clothe yourself in the Word of God, and you will not continue to struggle in the same way. *A new day is dawning for you!*

You can continue to work the same hours,
hang around with the same friends,
and spend your time haphazardly,
with no Word or power in you,
or you can challenge God
to provide you with a good job, friends,
and a way of life that will help you
draw closer to Him.
*If you do, you will walk
in a power greater than any you
have ever experienced!*

If My Words Abide in You...

*If ye abide in me, **and my Words abide in you,** ye shall ask what ye will, and it shall be done unto you* (John 15:7).

The second condition, we as believers must meet in order to receive the blessing of God, is for His words to abide in us.

If you only abide *in God*, but His Word does not abide

in you, then you'll wander around trying to figure out whether you are going to make it or not. But if you allow God's Word to abide in you, you will never be confused or defeated. If He abides in you, He will tell you who you are—a member of His royal priesthood and holy nation. Your flesh does not know who you are. It takes the Spirit of God in you to tell you that. And because you are a part of His kingdom, you will have confidence that God will supply all of your needs according to His riches in glory (Phil. 4:19).

Studying the Word

At first glance, some of the writings in the Bible may be confusing or hard to understand. Sometimes they may even sound contradictory, but they are not. That is why 2 Timothy 2:15 says,

> *Study to show thyself approved unto God, a workman that needeth not to be ashamed, rightly dividing the Word of truth.*

It is impossible for you to understand the Word and properly apply it to your life without first studying it. It contains the wisdom of God as He has revealed it to man. The Bible is the most important book you will ever read, so you must ask God to help you understand what it contains.

Instructions and revelations about everything you are ever going to receive in your life are in this book: *every anointing, gift, power, and blessing.* So why do we not have a natural desire to study the Bible? Why does it seem like a chore to us at times? The flesh cannot properly appreciate the things of the Spirit, so we must rise above our human nature to reach for all God has for us in His Word. Beyond that, the devil has deceived us into thinking the Word is too hard to understand. He knows he has lost you if you stand on the Word and say, "The devil lied to me for many years, but I am going to take everything God says in this book and I am going to own it and possess it. It is going to be mine. Bless God!"

Someone recently shared with me how the Lord helped her to reduce $40,000 in credit card debt to $5000. This amazing story occurred because she heard the truth in the Word and decided she could apply it to her life. She was tired of being broke and having creditors hound her. She took ownership of the Word and she said, "My debts are going down because I believe what the Word says!"

Right now every one of us is loaded with potential not only to pay off our debts, but to accomplish all that God has purposed for us from the very beginning. Healing, prosperity, revelation, and truth are available to those who have the Word of God abiding in them. But if it doesn't, you can be at the right place at the right time and still not receive power from God. You can come to church, say you are a Christian, and boast about how wonderful the sermon was, but that does not mean the power of God is in you and controls you. You may be *around* the Word, but do you *possess* the Word? People can go to church for 20 years and still not have any power.

For example, you can move from one country to another. But just because you are living in a new country does not mean you have become a citizen of it. You have the option to choose whether or not to become a citizen. You are in one country, but the country does not control you. Likewise, you can be in the Kingdom of God, but the Kingdom of God does not control you.

Here's another example—just because you have an account with a bank doesn't give you the right to make a withdrawal. You can open an account for $100, but it does not give you the authorization to write a check for $200. Your name is in the bank's computer, you have a check with your name and address on it, and the bank even has your Social Security number. But you better make sure when you write that check that you have enough money in the bank to cover it. In the same way, you can be in the Kingdom of God and want to draw from the Word of God, but you do not have enough power. Why? Because the Word, which gives you unlimited access to its riches, does not abide in you.

Do not feel proud when you go to church or say you are a born-again Christian. That does not move God. Yes, you abide in Him, you are living in Him, but it does not mean that His Word abides in you. That is why churches have problems that can even cause them to split. That is why people will not submit to authority. They are in Christ, but His Word is not in them. You can search, you can sit under the power, but still not be able to use the power.

The Process

Getting the Word of God to abide in you is a process; it does not happen overnight. Go back to 2 Timothy 2:15: "Study to show thyself approved." The word "study" suggests you must set aside some quality time. When you get alone, shut off the phone, television, and radio, then get a couple of books and research materials, and do some intense reading. When you study the Word, you have to approach it prayerfully, asking God to direct you in what He desires you to learn at that time. Sometimes it takes a while, but you must press on.

I can picture Paul saying to Timothy, "Make sure you go to a room by yourself and take time to study the Word. There are going to be times in your ministry when the enemy comes against you, when even church people attack you. Timothy, if you do not have the Word of God in you, your flesh is going to act up."

You, too, need to take time out to study the Word of God so when people are difficult on the job or when family members cause serious problems, you will be able to respond with wisdom from the Word coupled with His power residing in you. You will reap the benefits when the enemy comes against you, and you can say, "I know what the Word says, Satan. Take your tricks somewhere else."

After Jesus completed a 40-day fast, the devil approached Him. Jesus replied saying, "It is written...." Now some of us are also saying, "It is written," but the devil demands, "What is written?" At this point some of us feel helpless in not being able to quote the Bible because we have not spent enough time studying it. Studying takes time, and we can become too busy and neglect doing the very thing that will bring us life. We pass up the blessing of God's Word to spend time watching television or hanging out with friends.

In today's world, people are anxious whenever they run into problems. Why? The Bible says, "Be anxious for nothing" (Philip. 4:6). If we applied just that one scripture, do you know how much worry and stress we could avoid? We are ignorant of the Word that will change our lives when we approach it with faith.

Valuing the Word

If your heart is in something, you have a passion for it and spend a lot of time on it. You don't care what it takes. Some of you are so stuck on soap operas that you program your VCRs so you can watch them when you get home. Or because you are interested in someone, you will spend as much time as you can with him or her.

If God's Word is in you and you live in His Word, He will be your Lover. You should look forward to visiting the house of God to hear what your Lover has to say to you. You know God has a Word for you.

Wherever your treasure is, that is exactly where you are going to put your heart (Matt. 6:21). When a woman cashes her paycheck and puts the money in her purse, notice how close she holds her bag. Why? There is treasure inside.

We don't pay much attention to the Word of God because we don't value it as we should. We take good care of our car, our clothes, and our jewelry because we value them. *We need to place a much higher value on the Word of God.*

It is not enough to say you are a Christian. It is not enough to say that you go to church. It is not enough to say you bought the tape. It is not enough to say you have read a book written by Bishop Fernandez. It is not enough to say you went to "Manpower" or a "Woman Thou Art Loosed" conference. Just because you abide in God does not mean you will have the power. You should take time out with God to study and know how to use the Word in your everyday life. Get into the Word and wait upon the Lord. For they that wait upon the Lord shall renew their strength (Is. 40:31).

Changing Your Environment

And, being assembled together with them, commanded them that they should not depart from Jerusalem, but wait for the promise of the Father, which, said he, ye have heard of me.

For John truly baptized with water; but ye shall be baptized with the Holy Ghost not many days hence.

When they therefore were come together, they asked of him, saying, Lord, wilt thou at this time restore again the kingdom to Israel?

And he said unto them, It is not for you to know the times or the seasons, which the Father hath put in his own power.

But ye shall receive power, after that the Holy Ghost is come upon you: and ye shall be witnesses unto me both in Jerusalem, and in all Judea, and in Samaria, and unto the uttermost part of the earth. (Acts 1:4-8)

The disciples assembled themselves together in the Upper Room. This suggests they left one particular location and went to another. In other words, there was a change of surroundings that took place. Sometimes we need to step out in faith and leave where we are in order to make a step toward where we are going.

There was a time in my life when I got tired of watching other people around me getting blessed. I seemed to be doing the same things they were doing but all I heard were testimonies of their blessings, of the power they had, and of the overflowing of God in their lives. It led me to think, *God, what is wrong here? Are they serving a different God or is there something wrong with me?* I discovered there was something I was not doing. I tried to hear God in the wrong environment. I tried to pull the blessings from God down into the valley of depression where I dwelt, instead of moving into a place of faith in the Kingdom."

Let me explain further. God the Father could have sent the power of the Holy Spirit right where the apostles were. Jesus did not have to tell them to go to the Upper Room and wait for the power. He had them leave where they were in order to get them away from the other people who were full of doubt, fear, and confusion, so they could activate their faith. In the same way, I had to get away from the negative environment that had gotten me depressed in order to activate my faith. I had to "come away" and spend time in the Word.

If you are ever going to receive the power of God, you have to change your environment. What do I mean by your environment? You may have to change the way you think so you can have a renewed mind. You may have to change your friends. You may have to change your way of doing business. You may even have to change how you manage your time. There are only 24 hours in a day. I do not care what you do, God is not going to give you 25. If you are so busy that you have no time for the Word, no time to study, no time to pray, then you are too busy and something has to change.

Does that mean you have to quit your job or change your business hours? Will you have to find new friends or learn about time management? You have two choices.

Pick one. You can continue to work the same hours, hang around with the same friends, and spend your time haphazardly, with no Word or power in you, or you can challenge God to provide you with a good job, friends, and a way of life that will help you draw closer to Him. *If you do, you will walk in a power greater than any you have ever experienced!*

If you stay connected to Him through all
the winds and storms
that come your way, you will bear
much fruit and become truly
blessed and productive.
That is why He said you can ask what you
will, and it shall be given unto you.
You cannot remain in God
and not bear fruit.
The life that comes from the vine
will flow through the branches and result
in lasting fruit.

7

The Vine and the Gardener—
Putting It Together

I am the true vine; my Father is the gardener.

He cuts off every branch in me that bears no fruit while every branch that does bear fruit he prunes so that it will be even more fruitful.

You are already clean because of the Words I have spoken to you.

Remain in me, and I will remain in you. No branch can bear fruit by itself. It must remain in the vine. Neither can you bear fruit unless you remain in me.

I am the vine, and you are the branches. If a man remains in me and I remain in him, he will bear much fruit. Apart from me, you can do nothing.

If anyone does not remain in me, he is like a branch that is thrown away and withers. Such branches are picked up, thrown into the fire and burned. (John 15: 1-7)

*J*esus used the parable of the vine to help make the concept of abiding clear to the disciples. He explained to them that there are two types of Christians. There are branches (Christians) who are connected to the vine (God). Then there are others, who, at some point in time, have broken away from the vine.

You will find people who have made Jesus Christ their Lord and Savior, but eventually have allowed Satan to step in and break them away from the vine. These people think that because they are still in the church, because they attend services each week, pay their tithes and offerings, and support various ministries in the church, they are still connected to God. They may even read their Bible every now and then. However if you check on them a while later, you will find these people are not receiving life from the vine. It may be that the pressures of life have caused them to break away from the vine. They did not have enough substance or enough energy to brace themselves against the winds of life and the arrows of the enemy.

There will be seasons when the devil will go after you to test you. In those times you need to be able to say, "You can blow on me. You can tell me I am never going to be healed. You can tell me I am never going to get out of debt. But I am going to stay connected to the vine because *God promised me* that I will be more than a conqueror."

Those who stay connected to the vine do not allow winds of doctrine, other Christians, other people, or other issues to get them all bent out of shape. They do not wring their hands in despair when they run short of money one week. They do not allow the devil to tell them they cannot tithe because of their bills. The pressures of life do not disconnect them from the vine. They will not allow the enemy to tell them they cannot support the Kingdom of God with their tithes. And they will not allow the devil to tell them they cannot trust God.

When you are connected to the vine, you will trust in the Lord with all your heart and not lean on your own understanding (Prov. 3:5). You will not be moved by what society says. You will look to Him for the abundant provision that He has promised you.

The Lone Ranger Christian

Some of you are trying to be "lone rangers" and do it all on your own even though God has said you can do nothing apart from Him (John 15:5). You may think you can walk without Him, wink your eyes, stomp your feet, and nod your head without Him. Let me remind you the reason you can do all of these things is because God has decided to allow it. He breathed life into your body. He allowed you to wake up this morning and live one more day. You cannot do *anything* unless God allows it.

You would be a fool to let the devil trick you into believing that you can succeed quite nicely on your own. If you are not connected to the vine, you are going to wither and eventually die. You may look like a fine branch now and may even bear some fruit, but sooner or later your leaves are going to change color and your fruit will drop off. The things you used to do as a Christian, you will not want to do anymore. You will not have a desire to go to church. You will not have a desire to pray. You will not have a desire to read your Bible. You will not have a desire to push your way into His presence and say, "God I may be coming to You in broken pieces, but I am coming anyhow."

Jesus said that in order to receive the blessings of God, you cannot do it on your own. You must abide in Him and He in you; it cannot be one or the other, it must be both. For example, you can take a detached branch, hang it on a vine, and make it look as though it is connected to the vine. Just because it *looks like* it is connected to the vine, doesn't mean that it is. The leaves of the unconnected branch may be similar, so you can easily slip it in among the other branches. People who pass by may even be fooled. But before you know it, it will begin to wither and die.

Now what do you do with a branch when it falls from the vine? Do you leave it there? It's good for nothing, so you might decide to burn it. I believe the revelation Jesus wanted to give the disciples was that by not activating their faith and dwelling in the vine, they would allow themselves to be burned and trashed by the enemy.

Pruning Is Good for Us

God does not want us to get to the place where we become independent and disconnect ourselves from the vine because we are doing well. And so God has a process called "pruning." It helps us realize that our strength comes from the vine and not the leaves we have produced.

Branches that bear fruit have to be cut back, not to kill them, but to help them bear more fruit. What makes you think that when some of your leaves are being cut back that God is trying to punish you? What makes you think that when things are not going as you would like them to go, the enemy is on your back? How do you know that God is not pruning you? How do you know that God is not preparing you to bear more fruit?

We are people who like to have things go smoothly. We do not like the pruning. We are worried that God may cut our job off or the financial support that we depend upon. In reality, He is pruning us like the gardener prunes the vine. If all of the leaves remain, it will not have enough strength to bear fruit or resist the winds and storms that may come against it.

Withstanding the Hurricanes

If you abide in the vine, you don't have to worry about what winds the devil may blow. God will protect you in the midst of the storms of life. Do not be discouraged by the pressure that comes against you. You may be in a hurricane season. It may seem that after one hurricane leaves, another approaches: Hurricane Illness, Hurricane Lack of Finances, Hurricane Marriage Problems, Hurricane Rebellious Children, Hurricane Difficult Relationship—they all seem to be destroying you.

Sometimes your branches may be bent all the way to the ground, but *as long as you stay connected* to the vine, as soon as the wind passes, you will have enough strength to get right back into position where you belong. God promises: "He that dwelleth in the secret place of the most high shall abide under the shadow of the almighty" (Ps. 91:1). You will be safe because you have special protection from lasting harm.

If you stay connected to Him through all the winds

and storms that come your way, you will bear much fruit and become truly blessed and productive. That is why He said you can ask what you will, and it shall be given unto you. *You cannot remain in God and not bear fruit.* The life that comes from the vine will flow through the branches and result in lasting fruit.

Seek ye first the kingdom of God, and his righteousness; and all these things shall be added unto you. (Matt. 6:33)

If we are connected to Him, God pours everything into us. When the branch is connected to the vine, anything that comes from the vine can flow easily through the branch and feed it.

If we remain in Him and He in us, we can ask for blessings and He will send them to us. That means that God has given us a capacity large enough to hold everything we need to be fruitful. Some of us have limited ourselves. A branch will never cry out and say it cannot hold any more. A branch will never say, "Stop the flow." The branch has unlimited capacity—the more food the vine pumps into it, the more it absorbs.

When God created you, He placed in you a capacity you cannot fathom. God does not want you to just bear fruit. He wants you to bear *much* fruit. *You have a capacity that is much larger than you think you have. But once again, the key to access this capacity is faith.*

Some of us may say we are satisfied with half a glass of water. Some of us may be satisfied with one that's three-quarters full. Some of us may think that when our glass is full we have enough. But if we remain in Him and He in us, if we make ourselves available and make Him our Lord through faith, He will continue to pour an abundance into us. Our bodies will not be able to contain all He has for us. *God wants us to get more than full. He wants us to run over. He wants the anointing to flow; He wants us to be abundantly fruitful!*

.

You can become healthy and fit if you want,
but the realization of that dream
comes with fulfilling your responsibility.
It comes with eating right
and exercising.
*Your dreams are achieved
through fulfilling your responsibility
toward them.*
Without assuming the responsibility,
there is no success.

And It Shall Be Done Unto You

*If ye abide in me, and my Words abide in you, ye shall ask what ye will, **and it shall be done unto you*** (John 15:7).

Receiving the abundant blessings of God is really very easy. If you believe in your heart, confess what you believe, and remove any obstacles standing in your way, then receiving becomes the next logical step.

How do these principles of believing, confessing, and then receiving work in real life? For example, in order to be a successful businesswoman or man, you must first *believe* God has called you into the business and will help you succeed. Then start *confessing* it all the time—whether you are struggling (which usually occurs in the beginning) or not. If you put your faith in what God has said, you will receive His blessings.

You should follow the same procedure if you desire to have a successful marriage. Even if you and your spouse are having problems, begin believing that God desires your marriage to be blessed and then start confessing it is so. It's important not to think negatively or make critical remarks about your situation. By confessing positive statements, you're speaking in faith and abiding in Him and His Word. If you start believing and confessing, hold onto your hat—*you will begin to see the abundant provision that God has laid up for you!*

If you continuously and constantly "specialize in" walking by faith and take on the characteristics of the success you have learned about in the Word, before long, you will find yourself walking in success. For example, there are many Hollywood actors and actresses that we enjoy watching in the movies. Because they tend to play in the same type of movies over and over, they have developed a certain kind of character that we can identify. When a director seeks an actor for a particular role, he picks one who has successfully played similar roles in the past. For example, there are certain actors who specialize in romantic movies and others who specialize in action roles. Because they specialize in certain roles, they have become successful.

If you desire to be manager of a particular store and feel that God has called you to that position, you have to first start acting as if you already were the manager. You must be on time for work, dress appropriately, have a sincere concern for the company, and put in more effort than is expected of you. Before long, when the owner of the company looks at you he will "see" the *next* manager of his company. I'm not telling you to go to your job tomorrow and start acting as if you *are* the supervisor. You must wait for the promotion. What I mean is that *if you start acting as if you have the qualities of success within you*, those qualities will soon overtake you. It will not be a role you are playing. It will be your reality, something that truly depicts who you are.

I will use my personal story again to further explain. I had invited Bishop Earl Paulk from the Cathedral of the Holy Spirit in Atlanta, Georgia, to be the guest speaker at my church. Before he left, he looked at me and said, "Son, you have the ability to be a bishop. I want to ordain you." My first reaction was I didn't want the responsibility. I just wanted to be a pastor and concentrate on my church. I desired to expand our television ministry and continue writing books. In other words, I wanted to stay in my little corner so that everything would be safe.

But I had a divine appointment that day. The Lord spoke to me and said the anointing was upon my life from the time I was a little boy. The fact that Bishop Paulk asked me to become a bishop is a manifestation of what God placed in me. As a little child, even though I never wanted to become a pastor, I would act like one. I remember in Sunday School, they used to call me "the little reverend." People in my church saw the ability in me. Before Bishop Paulk came to our church, I was already doing things a bishop was supposed to do, but I didn't run out and try to get somebody to recognize me just so I could have the office of a bishop.

The manifestation of what you see in Henry Fernandez today actually began years before when I believed that God told me I was going to be a pastor. I unconsciously began doing the appropriate things God wanted me to do, that a pastor or bishop would normally do. The endorsement of a bishop came easily because I was already fulfilling the role *and enjoying it* because that is the call of God on my life. I believe God has moved on me to be a beacon of light in the 21st century, and my ministry is on the cutting edge, ready to explode. We will do things that will bring thousands of people into the kingdom of God and into the knowledge of the Lord Jesus Christ. And that will come about because we have faith in God and His Word.

Faith is the substance of things hoped for (Heb. 11:1). There has to be substance behind what you believe. If you are going to believe for a house, the substance of your faith for that house is your knowledge that you are supposed to have it, which gives you the power to obtain it. That word "power" is really talking about the ability you have to receive it. Receiving is easy today. Anybody can receive success, but you have to believe in what God has placed in your heart and act upon it.

Dreams Don't Have To Be Nightmares

To be successful, you must first dream. Some of you know what success is. You know where you want to go in life. You know what God has purposed for you, but you do not have it in your hand yet. You feel discouraged and think you are not successful, but success has to begin with your dream.

For example, success may have to do with your dream of getting married, or getting out of debt. Success may have to do with your dream of having a child or changing jobs or getting a promotion. If you do not have it yet, it is still a dream.

The only way you can motivate yourself to fulfill your dream is to believe God has given you the ability to do it. God is a rewarder of those who diligently seek Him (Heb. 11:6). Now if you diligently seek after your dream and tell yourself you can do it and believe in yourself, it gives you a *passion*. You will come alive and all of your thoughts and immediate desires will be tied to your dream. You can almost taste it, it's so real to you. When you talk about it, your whole body becomes animated. Your voice gets louder and your eyes sparkle. Any sacrifice you have to make to fulfill your dream seems small compared to what you envision will happen.

For example, let's say you want to buy a house, but at first you only talk about it. Talk is cheap. But then one day God puts the dream of home ownership into your heart. So you begin to believe He will make a way for you. Even though the obstacles are there, you must believe the house is yours. You realize your credit is bad. Even if you have to deny yourself some immediate pleasures right now, you do so because you have a dream. You work with your creditors and begin to repair your record. You work and scrimp and save for a down payment because you have a dream. You picture yourself living in the house. You are claiming your dream. You do not have it yet; it is still a dream, but you have begun to claim it.

All Things Are Possible

I have strength for all things in Christ who empowers me. I am ready for anything and equal to anything through him who infuses the inner strength in me. I am self-sufficient in Christ's sufficiency. (Philippians 4:13 Amplified)

The verse above says that when you believe that all things—including your dreams—are possible through Christ, *your belief in Him will empower you to succeed.* The Word of God says you can do all things through Christ because He is the one who will empower you to see your dream fulfilled. He gives you the ability; He gives you the strength. He gives you the way, the knowledge, the idea. He gives you the method and the direction to fulfill your dream. You will receive everything you need to make your dream a reality.

Robert A. Schuller, the author of the book entitled, *If It Is Going to Be, It Is Up To Me*, wrote in the introduction that the *dream of doing* leads to success. You may not like that *doing* word, but it leads to success and significance. So if you just say you "want to be" somebody, the only thing you will become is a "wanna-be." There are many people in this life who are wanna-bes. All they talk about is what they wanna-be, *not what they are becoming*. Dr. Schuller also said, "possibility plus responsibility equals success."

Just because all things are possible does not mean you will receive them. You won't get the house you dream about if you don't *do something*. You will not get out of debt if you do not *do something*. If you do nothing, this time next year you will be in the same position you are right now. Remember our discussion of moving mountains in chapter two? You have to move the obstacles out of your way so that you can receive all that God has for you. Can you imagine saying you want a child but you do not have sex with your wife? Can you imagine every night going to bed saying, "Good night, honey, and God bless"; yet you say you want to conceive a child? You must have an action plan in order to achieve your dream!

You can become healthy and fit if you want, but the

realization of that dream comes with fulfilling your responsibility. It comes with eating right and exercising. *Your dreams are achieved through fulfilling your responsibility toward them.* Without assuming the responsibility, there is no success. When many of you complain that you are not successful, it's because you are *riding on possibility and not working on your responsibility.*

It does not matter what you are going through. If you believe in the power of God and seek to know Him, you will see success in every area of your life.

Blueprint for Success

Now how do we get to success? Let's look at Psalm 119:15 in the Amplified Version.

I will meditate on thy precepts, and have respect to thy ways.

Through the Psalmist's *meditation* on God's ways, he received direction for his life. The Word of God will address *every area of your life.* If you spend a lot of time thinking about the ways of God, His instructions, and His teachings, God will help you map out a pathway for success in life.

The reason we cannot identify God's will and path for our lives and begin down the road toward success is because we are not meditating on Him. The person who meditates on the instructions and teachings of God will be like a tree firmly planted and tendered by streams of water, ready to bring forth its fruit in due season.

For he shall be like a tree firmly planted and tendered by the streams of water ready to bring forth its fruit in its season. Psalm 1:3

When you meditate on the Word of God, it allows you to bear fruit in your season. If you have an apple tree, it only bears apples during a particular season. It does not bring forth fruit all year round. So, why do you feel you should bear fruit all the time? Why do you feel you should bear fruit every day of your life, seven days a week, thirty-five days a month? No, I didn't make a mistake. I said thirty-five days a month because I wanted to show that sometimes God will allow us to bear fruit even when it is not our time. We expect God to always do it the way we think is right. We must remember that He is still God.

But there are other times when He allows you not to bear fruit. That doesn't mean you aren't useful. He has a use for you, but it is not yet your season to receive those things He has promised you. Therefore when you see your neighbor driving a new car, don't get jealous. It just happens to be their season and not yours.

When a man plants a tree, he does so in faith, believing the time will come when fruit will appear. But because of his dream, during the entire time before he sees any fruit, he continues in faith to water the tree, prune it, and protect it against insects. Then one day it brings forth the promised fruit in its season and he receives the promised blessing..

Remember, if you confess what you believe in your heart and do not doubt, *you will see the demonstration of the power of God in your life*. Your dreams come from your faith and are the beginning of your success!

There are things in this life that God
wants you to birth. *No one
else on the earth
can birth them but you.*
You must be sensitive to His timing.
You may wonder how long
your struggles will last.
The answer from God is that
*passion plus timing
equals success.*

Success

Blessed, happy, fortunate, prosperous is the man who walks and lives not in the counsel of the ungodly, following their advise, their plans and purposes, nor stands submissive and inactive in the path where sinners walk, nor sits down to relax and rest where the scornful and mockers gather.

But his delight and desire are in the law of the Lord and on his law, the precepts, the instruc-

tions, the teaching of God he habitually medi-
tates, ponders, and studies by day and by night.
(Psalm 1:1-2, the Amplified Version)

L et's talk more about success for a moment. You could describe a successful person as one who is "blessed, happy, fortunate, and prosperous." The Scripture gets at the heart of the matter and defines this person as one who doesn't walk in the counsel of the ungodly. In other words, the successful person abides in God and His Word and doesn't listen to those who don't.

Many of us are not successful or happy or prosperous because we spend more time listening to what the world (the ungodly) says than what God says. Our resulting lack of success creates frustration in our lives. We become depressed because we are not walking in faith. Years ago we sang a song in Sunday School that said, "Smile a while and give your face a rest. Raise your hand to the one you love the best. Then shake hands with those nearby and greet them with a smile." Today, we don't greet people with a smile. Why? Is life that bad? No, it's not—it's just that the majority of people are not walking in faith and so they have no belief that their circumstances will change. If you are walking in faith, you won't get rid of your problems with a wave of the hand, *but you can face them with a smile while God is working character into you.*

Your passion for your dream will lead you to the happiness you can have even when you have not yet seen any changes in your circumstances. Remember, passion plus timing equals success. You must believe that what you are working toward is your God-given dream. That will give you hope that God will indeed bring to pass what He has told you. You have to believe in your dream, even if you do not see it yet.

You are a success even before you have received the blessings that He has promised. A lot of people mistakenly believe success is an achievement of some sort and feel depressed when it hasn't happened yet for them. That isn't true success. Look at Bill Gates. He's not successful because he's worth billions of dollars. Bill Gates is successful because he believed in himself and used his abilities to design Microsoft Windows. The manifestation of his success is demonstrated in his wealth and is the end result of believing in himself. If you believe God has a plan for your success, confess it by faith and walk in it. You will be a success long before you ever see its manifestation.

Evidence of Things Not Seen

Now faith is the substance of things hoped for, the evidence of things not seen. Hebrews 11:1

Even if you have not yet seen the fulfillment of your dream, your belief and confidence in God will give you the assurance it is going to come to you. That is God's way. You don't have to see it to believe it when it is God speaking. We must walk not by sight, but by faith.

So if you believe God is going to give your dream to you, and you have a passion for it, you will experience it. If you desire to receive something from the Lord and you diligently seek after Him to get it and do not rush Him, God will fulfill His promise.

God's Timing

God's Word will accomplish what it was sent forth to do. The problem is in the timing. You may wonder how long you will have to wait. You may wonder how long your struggles will last. The answer from God is that *passion plus timing equals success.*

As you pray in faith daily, remind Him that He promised this dream to you. (If it does not come to pass, then it was not the Lord who gave you the dream.) But if God truly spoke to you about getting a house and a car, or about getting out of debt, or about entering a good marriage and having a family and a successful church; it must come to pass because God cannot lie.

When God spoke to me and told me He wanted me to become a pastor and be involved in world evangelism, I believed Him. He said it, and that was that. But it didn't come to pass overnight. However, I didn't simply sit down and wait for my dream to manifest itself. I did something about it. I listened for the voice of the Lord telling me the steps I needed to take along the way, and I faithfully followed them. I consecrated myself to the Lord and sought Him diligently.

I heard God tell me to plant a church and so I went out and did it. God said that before I was born, when I was in my mother's womb, He ordained me to become a pastor. So the birthing of The Faith Center did not "just happen" with me. It happened before the foundation of the earth. Even though many obstacles were against me, and it didn't look like it would ever come to pass, I continued to follow the words of the Lord. I didn't stop and accept defeat but continued to push ahead. Sometimes I felt very insecure about what I was doing. There were many other pastors who were more qualified than me. I told God I wasn't sure I could do it. I told God I didn't have the resources. But because God said it, I didn't doubt it would happen.

Only You Can Do It

There are things in this life that God wants you to birth. *No one else on the earth can birth them but you.* You must be sensitive to His timing. God said to plant the church, and we did. The timing was right for us, even though we didn't grow large overnight.

It was a struggle in the beginning, but I believed that God called me and I didn't have any hidden agendas of my own. I just wanted to serve God in the way He had planned all along. Even though there were problems upon problems, I knew this was the dream God gave me and I pursued it.

I learned to be patient as we discussed in chapter four. Even though my flesh was saying, "Come on, man, you should already have a congregation of 1000" when I only had a congregation of 50, I still knew God was going to fulfill the dream. Then He gave me a congregation of 1000. And God continued to work until now it is a congregation of more than 5000. God continues to bless me because I have faith in Him and the dream.

At one point I wanted to build a house; I believed I could build a fine one. My flesh warred against me, saying I was too ambitious. But I didn't have to steal any money to build it. I didn't need gimmicks to get it. I didn't ask anyone to mail money to me. I didn't beg for money. I knew I could build my home honestly. God fulfilled my dream because I knew how to seek Him diligently.

God fulfilled my dream because the timing was right. God fulfilled my dream because I had a passion for it. *God fulfilled my dream because I believed that He would!*

If God's Word tells you that you are
more than a conqueror,
then believe it and declare it.
That is how you activate the power
of God in your life.
God will not do anything until you
believe His Word,
until you *speak* His Word,
and until you
walk in His Word.

Faith Activates the Power of God

Therefore being justified by faith, we have peace with God through our Lord Jesus Christ:

By whom also we have access by faith into this grace wherein we stand, and rejoice in hope of the glory of God.

And not only so, but we glory in tribulations also: knowing that tribulation worketh patience;

And patience, experience; and experience, hope:

And hope maketh not ashamed; because the love of God is shed abroad in our hearts by the Holy Ghost which is given unto us. (Romans 5:1-5)

How can you get the power of God working in your life? How can you get God to act on your behalf and bring you success? How can you get God to move in your circumstances? The answer is by activating your faith. We have already discussed faith quite a bit. Remember, according to Hebrews 11:1, "Now faith is the substance of things hoped for, the evidence of things not seen."

The Word of God tells us that our faith is a "right now" kind of faith. Faith is not hope. Hope deals with something that comes in the future. You do not have to wait until the battle is over to rejoice and declare yourself successful. By faith you can declare yourself a winner *now* in the midst of all your circumstances. Regardless of what you are going through, by faith you declare yourself to be an overcomer both now and in the future.

When I say confess it now, I mean you must tell yourself, "I don't see the blessings yet, I don't see my miracle yet, but I thank God for my job. I don't see it yet, but I thank Him for my health. I don't see it yet, but I thank Him for my financial breakthrough. I don't see it yet, but I thank Him in advance for those things He has ordained for my life."

The Bible also tells us that faith cometh by hearing and hearing by the Word of God. In order for you to receive faith, in order for your faith to be activated and for you to walk in faith, you must be informed about faith. This means you must hear the Word of God over and over.

Many people don't activate their faith because their faith isn't based on the Word of God. When the Word tells us that faith is the substance of things hoped for, the evidence of things not seen, it means if we believe God *now* for the things we hope for, we *will see* the evidence of it.

What You Hear Will Affect Your Life

To activate your faith, you have to fill your mind with the positive words it contains. If you hang around negative people, your mind will be filled with negative thoughts, and you will become a negative person yourself. But God has a much better life in mind for you. God wants you to think positively. He wants you to walk by faith and not by sight. In other words, God doesn't want you to look at your present circumstances as the final result, He wants you to *believe in Him who can make the impossible things become possible.*

If your friends always confess how broke they are and how much they are in need of more money, then your mind is going to be programmed to believe that is a normal way of thinking about finances. But if you become friends with people who are positive thinkers and talkers, you will begin to tell yourself that your God shall supply all your needs according to His riches in glory. You'll begin to speak and confess the Word of God for your finances. You'll begin to see a distinct change in your finances, and your faith in the Word of God is what will have changed them.

Faith Is Based on God's Promises

Faith is not based on what you can see, but on the *promises of God*. Stop looking at your circumstances and begin to look at the Word of God. If God's Word tells you that you are more than a conqueror, then believe it and declare it. That is how you activate the power of God in your life. God will not do anything until you *believe* His Word, until you *speak* His Word, and until you *walk* in His Word.

If you want God to act on your behalf, you must look God straight in the face and say to Him, "You said it in Your Word. You have made promises in this book, the Bible. You told me from Genesis to Revelation that I am a blessed seed. The promises You made to me are written in the Book. If I take hold of Your Word, whatever You speak into my life will not return until it is accomplished." When you remind God of His Word, God will send help to you.

Our success is not by works that any man should boast. *It is not you who will change your circum-*

stances, but it is the Holy Spirit who is working through you. It doesn't matter how many years it has been since you received the Holy Spirit. Time has nothing to do with how powerful you will become and how ably you will handle issues in your life. It really boils down to the Holy Spirit who is working through you. If your faith is activated, He is the one who is going to accomplish the task through you. Many people believe that because they are filled with the Holy Spirit, they have the power to change the world by their own gifts. On the contrary, it is Christ who lives within you and is working through you who will accomplish anything of value in your life.

No Word, No Faith, No God

How can you desire a change in your negative circumstances and want them to become positive experiences if you don't know God? The Bible says "In Him we live" (Acts 17:28). In other words, everything about your life should be centered in God. Every thought that is in your mind should be based on the Word of God. My whole life should be ordered by the Lord. Whatever you and I do in this life should be done in the power of His Word.

When you truly get a revelation from the Bible and understand more fully what it means, your faith will move the hand of God. God wants you to walk by faith. He wants you to confess His Word and operate in faith.

He wants you to move from faith to faith, from victory to victory.

Change the way you talk. Stop speaking negatively and your mind will begin to think positively. Confess positive declarations from the Word of God and your faith in God will become stronger. God wants you to leave those negative ideas behind and begin to believe His Word and begin to operate as if your circumstances have already changed. Deal with the issues of life in faith. Tell the devil that God is going to move mountains out of your life now. (See chapter two for a fuller discussion of this topic.)

> *If you have faith as a grain of mustard seed, you shall say unto this mountain, Remove hence to yonder place; and it shall remove; and nothing shall be impossible to you.* (Matthew 17:20)

There are circumstances in your life that the devil wants you to push under the table and not deal with. But God wants you to handle them right now. I encourage you today to use your faith. Tell that particular situation in your life that God is taking care of it; God has answered your prayers and you believe He is going to turn this negative situation into a positive one. It is going to become something that will bring glory to Him. Then watch and see God work in your life!

Operating in the Power of Faith

How do you know if you are going to make it? Because the Word and your faith declare it! First Thessalonians 5:8 tells us that you are to prepare yourself.

But let us, who are of the day, be sober, putting on the breastplate of faith and love; and for an helmet, the hope of salvation.

Please note what it says at the beginning of that verse: "But let us, who are of the day..." It is very important for you to understand that "the day" is the time at hand. We are talking about right now, the very moment you are faced with. The Word of God says we must take up the armor of faith *now*.

The armor of faith can be likened to the clothes we put on each morning before we start the day. The Word of God tells us that even before we are faced with the problems or difficulties of the day, we must put on faith. We know there is a task out there facing us, and we must prepare for it by clothing ourselves with God's power.

The Bible itself is ineffective if the words on the pages don't get into your heart, mind, and spirit. If you don't feed on them, the words will have no effect on your life. The Word of God must take effect if you are to be successful. The more you hear the Word, the more you can put it into your mind and feed on it. Then you'll begin to operate according to what the Word is telling you to do.

Many Christians lack a hunger to learn about God's character and His will for their lives. Ten years ago, I took it upon myself to get into the Word of God and study it to learn more of Him. Let me liken it to a soldier who is going out to war. He has to arm himself with many types of weapons because he doesn't know how he is going to be attacked. He doesn't know which weapons will be directed at him so he must prepare himself for any and all types of warfare. If we take the Word of God and get it into our minds and let ourselves be saturated with it, we will be prepared for anything the enemy can throw at us. There are no demons and no spiritual forces in high places that can ever conquer us. We're prepared with our faith and so we can quench every fiery dart of the enemy.

Unfortunately, today there are people who walk right into the enemy's camp without properly arming themselves. They believe that calling themselves Christians and joining a church are enough to qualify them to be covered and to be shielded from the attack of the enemy. In reality, what the devil fears is the Word of God because it is quick and sharp. It is powerful enough to cut through any demonic forces. It will stop every fiery dart the enemy can throw at you. *It is not a system, not a religion, it is the Word.*

We must get committed to studying the Word of God and applying it to our lives. We must believe it and act on it. It is not a system or formula where you say this is how it always works, one, two, three. No. You read the Word; study it, apply it, and then activate it.

When I began to walk in the power of faith, I found that the faith I have in the Word of God is strong enough to move any mountain! Let me share one of the times when God worked on my behalf. I needed approximately $175,000 in three months. Our ministry's lease was up on a particular building, and they had already sold it to another church. I needed $175,000 for renovation costs, etc. to move to a new location. When I looked at the church's financial records, it was not encouraging at all. There was nothing in them that told me our church could meet a challenge like that.

But I took the Word of God, and I challenged Him. I said, "God, I'm not doing this on my own. In fact, if it were left up to me, I would not even be a preacher. But You called me. You told me You would see me through to the end. You told me that if I walked in obedience, You would bless me. Now I am not asking You for a comfortable lifestyle. I am not asking you to keep me from tests and trials because I understand that nobody will ever escape them. But right now, God, I'm at a particular point where I don't have anywhere else to go. I don't have a place to put the people you have given me to oversee. This is your work. You assigned this job to me. Now the Bible says the words You speak will not return void. They will accomplish everything which they were sent forth to do. Now God I am believing that You are going to work on my behalf."

The moment I said that, God spoke a Word into my life reassuring me He would do it. He reminded me of the verse, "He that began a good work in you will perform it until the day of Jesus Christ" (Phil. 1:6). If I didn't know the Bible, God probably wouldn't have spoken that to me because it came in the form of a scripture that I remembered.

Hearing the Word is the only way faith can be activated in your life. Hearing the Word will bring forth faith. Hearing the Word will bring the voice of God to you. You cannot just hear Him by praying. He will speak to you through prayer, but He wants you to talk to Him through His Word. When you remind Him of His Word, He remembers. When you open the Bible and begin to read the Scriptures, God is actually speaking to you and that is how your faith can be developed.

My faith was increased when I believed God for that $175,000. God showed me through Habakkuk 2:2 to write the vision down and make it plain. Write it upon tables so the people can read it and run with it. God gave me that Word, and I had faith in the Word. I went to my congregation and read this scripture and shared what the Lord was saying. In three months, less than 300 people gave $175,000 cash to the ministry. This was up-front money that I needed in order to renovate the new building that we were moving into. Now that is faith!

I could tell you story after story of how God has moved in my life when I activated my faith. He moved on my behalf because I opened His Word and spoke His

Word into the circumstance, regardless of how bad it looked. The prophet Elijah asked in Ezekiel 37:3, "Can these bones live again?" The answer was "Yes, Lord, they can live." I don't care how dead your situation looks today, *if you speak the Word of God into that situation, the Word of God will bring life to it!*

Do something you have never
done before.
Step out of the norm.
Get away from your comfort zone.
Start taking risks.
Believe that God wants to bless you
and take the risk. Step out by faith
and stand on His Word.
If He says you are going to be successful,
then go after success.
While you go after success, the blessings of the
Lord will make you rich.

Access by Faith

Therefore being justified by faith, we have peace with God through our Lord Jesus Christ:

By whom also we have access by faith into this grace wherein we stand, and rejoice in hope of the glory of God. (Romans 5:1-2)

God's original intention for mankind was that we have life and have it more abundantly. Man was created to declare the glory of God, but along the way we messed up and needed salvation.

Thankfully, God in His mercy has redeemed us. In these verses the Apostle tells us we are justified by faith and have peace with God through our Lord Jesus Christ who pleaded our case and made peace with God for us through His sacrifice on the cross. It is faith in Jesus that gives us access once again into the promises of God.

Faith Gives Us Opportunities

None of us deserve to stand in the presence of an awesome God, but by faith we have the opportunity to do so. The promises are there and all we must do is access them by faith. Whatever you dream, whatever you believe God for today, you can access by faith. If you believe it is yours, according to the Word of God, you shall receive it. If you believe God has promised you prosperity, you can access prosperity by faith. If God promised you healing, you can access healing by faith. If God promised you a successful marriage, you can access that successful marriage by faith.

If according to His Word He promised you that you are going to be a successful businessperson, then access that by faith. If He promised you that He would give you the ability to create wealth by becoming an entrepreneur, then access that by faith. There is nothing that is impossible to God. *All things are possible if you have faith.* Those things that you believe Him for today, you can receive if you access them by faith.

Before we became Christians, before we confessed our sins, we had no access to the riches of His Kingdom. We had no access to prosperity, health, or success. We had no access to a good marriage, good relationships with our kids, family, and friends. But because we are now connected to God, He has blessed us and seated us in heavenly places. Through His Son Jesus Christ, He has given us access to all those things. I pray that you will begin to confess success for your life and begin to access those things you have been waiting around for God to give you. All you have to do is access it by faith. If He said it, believe it, and walk in it.

I want to share another story of how, by faith, I accessed the blessings of God. It involves our present building location. I was believing God for $1.6 million, and I just didn't know where this money was going to come from. We wanted to purchase the property and we simply didn't have the funds. But I believed God. I again went to Him and I spoke the Word into that situation. I said, "God, this is not my doing. I didn't want it. Now I'm walking according to Your Word. I believe You are *not* a God who lies, so I'm going to trust You. I'm going to remain faithful. God, I believe that this property is ours and I believe that even when banks are saying, "No" to us, You are saying "Yes" to us. You have already worked it out. You knew our ending before our beginning, so now I'm going to walk in faith."

In less than two months, God sent a stranger my way who was able to make a deposit of $1.6 million for us without any hassle. Now that's God! That's accessing the favor of God. That's accessing the blessings and the promises of God by faith. Now if I didn't believe it, I wouldn't have challenged God. If you challenge God for what you believe, He will act on His Word.

The Access Door

Romans 5:2 says we have access by faith into this grace and a door of opportunity through the blood of Jesus Christ. Satan will try to tell you that you are not what God intended you to be...you'll never become successful...you'll never see the power of God in your life. Many of us believe that lie. If we stand on the Word of God, however, and begin to access the things of God by faith, He will release them to us.

A lot of people have problems with those who talk about prosperity, especially preachers. Of course I don't agree with preachers who work on your emotions, trying to get money from you. But when preachers with integrity begin to teach these biblical truths without expecting to receive anything from us, God's people need to listen.

You must release your faith and the blessings will be

released into your life. For example, if you want a financial blessing in your life in order to get out of debt, pay your bills, and not have to worry about where money is coming from, then you have to release your faith. You have to access prosperity by faith. Many people just look at the concept, but they don't walk in the reality. Until that money is deposited into your account, it's not yours. So many Christians are wishing for it. But God is not a God of wishes; He is a God of reality. He is all powerful and He can release the riches of His kingdom into your life in an instant.

How do you access prosperity? You have to *follow what the Word says.* According to Malachi 3:10, we must first bring our tithe into the storehouse. The storehouse is your local assembly, the place where you are fed on a weekly basis and are taught the Word of God. And according to Matthew 6:33, you access prosperity when you *seek God and His kingdom and His righteousness.* He said, "...all these other things shall be added unto you." You must first seek God. Make God number one on your list. When you seek Him above all else, then you will be given everything you need. Money is not a problem. You will receive it, but you have to seek Him first.

Then Luke 6:38 tells us to give and it shall be given unto us. That is another aspect of how you access prosperity. *You cannot get anything until you give.* I am not just talking about giving to a church. Giving can also involve bringing a pair of shoes to your neighbor or feeding a meal to a homeless person.

Give and it shall be given unto you pressed down, shaken together, running over shall men also give unto your bosom. (Luke 6:28)

God uses people to distribute His wealth. When you sow into the kingdom of God, when you sow into God's purpose for your life, God says that *He will use people on the earth to turn around and bless you.* He will give you favor with them.

If you are sick and you want to be in health, how do you access health? You have to *stand on the promises in the Word of God.* You have to access it by the Word. When the Word tells you that by His stripes you are healed, that alone should tell you that God, through His Son Jesus Christ, paid the price and destroyed sickness at Calvary for you. Now you, by your belief and faith, can walk in divine healing.

If you want to access success, whether it be in your career or business, you can access it. The Bible says that God wants you to be successful. He wants to bless you. If He said He wants to bless you, don't worry about it, just walk in it and access it by faith. When you learn to walk in strong faith and access the success of God for your life, it will blow your mind. *I encourage you not to let your time on earth end without fully accessing everything God intended for you.*

First You Move, Then God Will Move

Ask, and it shall be given you, seek, and you shall find, knock, and it shall be opened unto you. (Matthew 7:7)

In order for you to experience all that God has for you, you must make the first move in faith, then God will respond with the fulfillment of promises from His Word. Otherwise, His power will never be activated to the fullest extent in your life. Do something you have never done before. Step out of the norm. Get away from your comfort zone. Start taking risks. Believe that God wants to bless you and take the risk. Step out by faith and stand on His Word. If He says you are going to be successful, then go after success. While you go after success, the blessings of the Lord will make you rich. But you must remember it is a *process which you have to go through in order to get rich, receive health, and be blessed.*

If you don't step out in faith toward success, then you have already pronounced failure over yourself. The enemy wants you to sit there and tell yourself, "Well, it worked for somebody else, but it can't work for me." If you allow the Word of God to work and take root in your heart and grow, you will see the fruits that God has purposefully planned for your life. *He gets pleasure out of seeing you become successful.* Surprised? Let me repeat that sentence. *God gets pleasure out of seeing you become successful.* Fantastic!

When you make the first move, God will make the next one. His Word searches the earth for people who will dare Him, for people who will say, "God, You said this. Because You said it, and You cannot lie, I believe you are going to do it for me." If you do that, God will step into your environment. He will step into your circumstances, and He will change your situation. *And you will never be the same again!*

I pray that the Holy Spirit will open
your understanding
so that you can have great faith.
You can have the blessings of God
if you want them. They are available to you.
They will not come easy;
you have to be persistent.
You may even need to be desperate.
*Do something you have never done before
and watch God move
in your life today!*

Persistent Faith

And, behold, men brought in a bed a man which was taken with a palsy: and they sought means to bring him in, and to lay him before him.

And when they could not find by what way they might bring him in because of the multitude, they went upon the housetop, and let him down through the tiling with his couch into the midst before Jesus.

And when he saw their faith, he said unto him, Man, thy sins are forgiven thee.

And the scribes and the Pharisees began to reason, saying, Who is this which speaketh blasphemies? Who can forgive sins, but God alone? But when Jesus perceived their thoughts, he answering said unto them, What reason ye in your hearts?

Whether is easier, to say, Thy sins be forgiven thee; or to say, Rise up and walk?

But that ye may know that the Son of man hath power upon earth to forgive sins, (he said unto the sick of the palsy,) I say unto thee, Arise and take up thy couch, and go into thine house.

And immediately he rose up before them, and took up that whereon he lay, and departed to his own house, glorifying God.

And they were all amazed, and they glorified God, and were filled with fear, saying, We have seen strange things to day. Luke 5:18-26

Persistent faith receives what it needs from God and it refuses to be deterred by obstacles that may be in the way. It brings the power of God into your life.

If you want to see the manifested Word of God, your

faith has to be strong. Not only should your faith be strong, but you must be persistent in it. You have to push until something happens. You cannot just say, "God, I believe you," and then quit. The devil will quickly test you to see if you believe what you just said. So you must have a faith that doesn't quit.

Persistent faith will allow you to receive from God when other people are not. Have you ever wondered why Jesus could step into a particular environment and only heal one person while leaving the others untouched? Think about that. It's all about persistent faith.

Let's look at the biblical story about the woman who had been subject to bleeding for a long time. She had gone to doctors for more than 12 years, and they couldn't solve her problem. The woman heard that Jesus was passing by and she made her way to Him, to where the blessing was, and where the anointing was flowing. She received her healing while the others who were there did not. You can be right in the midst of the healing power of God and still not be touched by it. It's all about how persistent you are in your faith.

How Persistent Are You?

How serious are you in getting what God has ordained for you? Are you going to just sit back and say, "God whichever way you want to bless me, just bless me? I do not know how You are going to do it, God, I will just wait on you. I will sit here and have a little pity party and hopefully You will come through for me." That is not persistent faith. Persistent faith says, "I don't care who is around Him, I don't care who has put in a request, I will continue to go to Him until I get my miracle."

Even though people tried to stop the woman with the bleeding problem from seeing Jesus, she was persistent. She said, "If I could just touch the hem of His garment..." That is how persistent this woman was. She felt all she needed to do was touch something that was touching Him. *And she was right, because she did it in faith.*

Some of you want God to send an angel down to shine a bright light on you. Some of you say you want to see Jesus for yourself. You want to touch Him and put your fingers in His scarred hands as Thomas did. But you don't have to see Jesus to believe what His Word says.

Whatever it is you want from God, how persistent will you be to ask Him for it? Are you just going to sit there and say, "Well, Lord, if it comes, it comes. If it happens, it happens." This isn't persistence. Regardless of the obstacles, you have to tell yourself, "You know what, I am going to get my blessing!"

The woman knew the entire town was aware of her problem.. But, she really didn't care. Everybody was talking about her anyway. Everyone was saying, "Don't touch that woman. She is unclean."

But the woman was desperate. She had seen all the

doctors in her area, and they had been unable to do anything for her. She said, "You know what, you can't help me. I'm going to try Jesus." The woman threw her pride away. Can you imagine how they reacted toward her when she was making her way through the crowd? I believe most of them were probably trying not to touch her. Sometimes when people are trying to shun you, God uses it to make a clear path for you to get to Him! Don't get bent out of shape when people try to isolate you and treat you unkindly. God is setting you up for a miracle. In fact, God sometimes needs to move people out of your life to give you the blessing. Although the crowd scorned this woman, their hatred made the way to Jesus much easier. She never pushed anyone out of the way. They pushed themselves back. She came to Jesus, and all of a sudden, the crowd parted because they didn't want to touch her.

If you're persistent, if you overlook what the boss is doing to you on the job, if you overlook what your coworkers are doing to you, if you overlook what the enemy has put before you, and you stand firm on the Word of God with persistence, you'll get to God and receive His blessings much easier.

The woman told Jesus that for 12 years the doctors had not been able to solve her problem. She was desperate. The reason so many of us don't receive from the Lord is because we are not desperate enough. When you become desperate, you become persistent. This woman probably thought to herself that Jesus was the last hope she had. *If He won't do it, then nobody can do it. What do I have to lose if I go to Jesus?*

Today, what do *you* have to lose if you are persistent with your faith? Persistent faith will do for you what it was intended to do for everyone.

With God All Things Are Possible

In Luke 5, we see the story of a man who couldn't walk. The Bible says he and his friends heard that Jesus was in the house with a group of people who also were sick. Because of the great crowd, the lame man couldn't get into the house where Jesus was ministering the anointing and the power of His healing. The Bible says his friends wanted to tell Jesus that he needed healing, but they couldn't get near Him because of all the people. They came up with a creative solution because they desperately wanted him to be healed. Those men were persistent in their faith.

> *And when they could not find by the way they might bring him in because of the multitude, they went upon the housetop. . (Luke 5:19)*

Picture yourself as one of the lame man's friends that day. Many of us would have said, "Well, I guess we might just as well go home because the place is too crowded.

We can't get our friend in there. We'll have to bring him back another day." Many of you would have walked away. How many blessings have you walked away from because you were not persistent?

Do you really want to get out of debt? Sometimes our biggest problem is that we are trying to *act like we already have the blessings.* God is trying to give them to us, but He wants us to get to the place where we acknowledge we do not have them. If we can admit it and be persistent to go after them, He will give them to us. But because we act like we already have them, we don't see the need of doing anything extraordinary in order to get them.

The Bible says they couldn't find a way at first to get the lame man inside, but they were persistent. This man had some powerful people around him. These are the kind of people I want around me. Other people who didn't have the same persistent faith might have taken the man home when they couldn't get him inside. But his friends decided they would find a way to get him to Jesus, even though there seemed to be no way.

I want friends like that who say, "With God all things are possible," and who remind me, "I can do all things through Christ who gives me the strength" (Phil. 4:13). Don't tell me that I can't! Greater is He who is in me than he who is in the world (1 Jo. 4:4). If God did it yesterday, He will do it again today. If God did it for the lame man, He can do it for me too.

We are people who have been trained to go in by the normal entrance. The door is here, the window is there, and we feel these are the only ways to enter a place. But God has a blessing for you and *He wants you to find a way to get it.* Even though the enemy says the door is closed, God says you do not have to go through the regular door of blessing; you can go through the roof; you can go through people who do not even like Him. You *can* find a way to get the blessing from Him.

God Will Find a Way

Almighty God will find a way to bless you. If the IRS can always find you to send your tax bill, don't tell me that my God, who knows all things, can't find a way to send you a blessing. Don't let the crowds stop you. Don't let locked doors stop you. God wants to bless you abundantly, but you have to be persistent.

I'm a firm believer that my blessings will come whether the enemy wants them to or not. Sometimes God won't send them through the door. He has other ways to send the blessing. He may even cut an opening through the roof. God says, "When I get ready to bless you, I can cut a doorway anywhere I want to cut it. I will bless you where and how I want to bless you. If I want to put the doorway in the roof, that's my business."

Can you imagine all of the people who were there in the house? All it would have taken was for them to just reach out and touch Him to receive their healing. They were so close to the Healer. But it took a man who came through the most unlikely place of all to get His attention. Some of us are in the very presence of God, yet we do not touch Him.

Sometimes you have to do something extraordinary to receive God's blessings. If you want to touch Him, you can't just sit there and say, "Well, I have been saved for 22 years. Thank you, Jesus. I praise your name, Lord. I have been in the church all my life. Praise the Lord."

You may have to do something that will get His attention. So, all of a sudden, Jesus looked up and saw that these people had cut a hole in the roof. The one who got Jesus' attention was the one who was persistent. When they lowered him down, Jesus turned to him and began to minister to him because of his persistent faith.

How Desperate Are You?

Desperation, I believe, will create ingenuity. When you get desperate, you will do things you would never do otherwise. It doesn't matter how quiet you are, it doesn't matter how sophisticated you think you are. There are people who softly praise the Lord. But if their house is on fire and they are locked up in it—desperation will make them come out of character and shout for help.

Desperation will make you do some very unusual things. Before you know it, you become very creative, doing what you never thought you would do. That is what the lame man's friends did. They probably said, "We have to get him to Jesus. How do we do it? Let's go up to the roof and cut a hole!" How much more should we as children of faith begin to think that all things are possible if we believe!

The kind of friends I want around me are people who will say, "Bishop, all things are possible." Jesus saw the faith they had for their friend. Then He spoke to the one who was coming through the ceiling saying, "Thy sins are forgiven thee." Did the man go there for salvation? No! He simply wanted to walk. But because of their persistent faith, he got much more than he bargained for. Not only did he receive his healing, he received salvation as well. Sometimes God gives us even more than we ask of Him.

The people in the house said Jesus spoke blasphemy because only God can forgive sins. The friends of the lame man didn't have the unbelieving attitude they did. If the man had been carried into the house, the people's unbelieving attitude there might have influenced him and kept him from receiving the blessing. It's important who your friends are. Thankfully the people who carried him onto the roof were people of strong faith.

Maybe the way you are trying to gain faith today is not the way you ought to go about doing it. Let's say you want to get out of debt. You can borrow money to pay back what you borrowed in the past, but that will not solve the problem—that only gets you in deeper so that you must borrow more to pay back what you borrowed, to pay back what you borrowed!

God simply says, "Trust me." Now faith is not that hard. Just cut a hole through the roof. Start doing something that you have never done before in faith. Be persistent. I know what the doctors are saying to you, but be persistent. The doctors are doing their job, but whose report are you going to believe? You should believe the report of the Lord. That is persistent faith.

If you're persistent in your faith, God will give you the desires of your heart (Ps. 37:4). Sometimes you must get desperate in order to receive it. How many of you would easily agree to be taken up to the rooftop? Or instead, would you insist that your mother didn't train you to behave that way? Desperation will cause you to do things you have never done before.

Let me tell you a story about my wife. I'm going to show you what desperation does to a person. My wife is a very sophisticated, high-class kind of lady, and there are certain things she just will not do. During her pregnancy, we made a trip to Miami. I had to park the car quite a distance from where we were staying. As we walked back to the car, she became tired and said, "You know what, I can't make it. Please go get the car for me."

I gladly ran to get the car, but when I drove back to where I had left her, I didn't see her. As I continued looking, I finally saw my wife sitting on the sidewalk. She was eating an ice cream cone she had bought from a stranger in one of those little trucks. I wanted to run home for my camera, it was such an unusual sight!

I couldn't believe it—my wife sitting on a street corner? That was totally out of character for her. But, she was pregnant, and she didn't care what anyone thought. Those of you who have been pregnant know what I'm talking about. A pregnant woman will do things she has never done before when she begins to feel desperate.

I pray that the Holy Spirit will open your understanding so that you can have great faith. You can have the blessings of God if you want them. They are available to you. They will not come easy; you have to be persistent. You may even need to be desperate. *Do something you have never done before and watch God move in your life today!*

Strong faith means naming the thing
you want and then patiently
waiting until the time comes to receive it.
It is knowing that you have it
stored up for you and then waiting for the
God-appointed time to withdraw it.
Strong faith gets you on the receiving end.
This is what Abraham did.
He waited in faith over the years to receive
what he had been promised.

Strong Faith Glorifies God

(As it is written, I have made thee a father of many nations) before him whom he believed, even God, who quickeneth the dead, and calleth those things which be not as though they were.

Who against hope believed in hope, that he might become the father of many nations, according to that which was spoken, so shall thy seed be.

And being not weak in faith, he considered not

his own body now dead, when he was about a hundred years old, neither yet the deadness of Sarah's womb:

He staggered not at the promise of God through unbelief; but was strong in faith, giving glory to God. (Romans 4:17)

Before I can explain what "strong faith" is, I first need to explain what it *is not*. Strong faith is not *a repeated confession* where you say something over and over again, trying to convince yourself that you believe. Many people think they have strong faith because of the number of times they recite a scripture verse. *Strong faith is not repeated confession.*

Strong faith is not name it and claim it. So many Christians are frustrated today because they have this impression that God is supposed to give everything to them *right now*. They think as soon as they name the blessing they should be able to see it poured into their lives. If it doesn't happen right away, they get disappointed. They complain to God that He is not doing what He said He would do.

For example, you might hear someone say, "God, I believe that your Word says we will be prosperous." You claim that promise for your life and expect it to happen immediately. You expect to receive money or wealth right away. You sit at home waiting for the "prize patrol" to knock on your door and hand you a million dollar check. You imagine that an insurance check from an un-known friend or relative will be delivered to your house. Your mind has been conditioned to name it and claim it. But that is not strong faith. That is *walking in ignorance*.

Strong faith is not an expression of outward emotion. For example, some people try to sing songs to convince themselves that the Lord will make a way somehow. So they sing a lot of songs to reassure themselves. Instead of singing songs *in faith*, they sing in order to *drum up faith*.

Others believe that tears can bring about strong faith—the more you cry, the stronger your faith. That is just not so. Some believe that if they jump a few times in church and get emotional, or *express their worship outwardly* in some way they will demonstrate to others that they have strong faith. Once again, it's not true.

All of these actions are outward attempts to make you *feel like you have strong faith*, but they do not flow from your spirit.

Convincing Confession

Now, what is strong faith? Strong faith is demonstrated by a *convincing confession*. A convincing confession is walking through a difficult situation and declaring that you will still stand firm on God's promise no matter what happens next. You don't argue about the situation or pretend it doesn't exist. You don't have to convince yourself God is going to make a way for you because you *believe* it. You know that if God promised you these things, you *will* receive them. Even when everything around you seems to be the opposite of what you are declaring, strong faith means being convinced that God will work things out. It doesn't matter what anyone else says; what counts is what God has said.

Name It and Wait

Strong faith means you have the power and the ability to *name* what God says in His Word and then *wait* for it to come to pass. This is just the opposite of "name it and claim it." Strong faith means you can wait on God after you name the promise and say, "God, I believe you for this thing and I believe you for this promise. I am not going to rush You because you have everything lined up to happen in the proper time. I believe You. I don't know *when* and I don't know *how*, but I do know *that* somehow, someday, You *are* going to bring it to pass."

The waiting period is something we don't like to hear about. We don't enjoy having to wait for anything. That is why society uses credit cards. But there is a different kind of credit discussed in the Bible. Let's take a look at Romans 4:23 (NIV).

The Words "it was credited to Him" [speaking of Abraham] *were written not for him alone, but*

also for us, to whom God will credit righteous-
ness for us who believe in him who raised Jesus
our Lord from the dead.

Everything that Abraham was going to receive was already credited to him. *That credit is the opposite of the*
credit cards of today. When it says that it was credited
to him for righteousness, that credit was based on
Abraham's faith in God. God had already stored up the
blessings for Abraham. He opened a special account for
Abraham and then deposited something in it. Over the
process of time, Abraham could withdraw from it. It is
really more like a savings account which contains money
you have already deposited. You have free access to
withdraw what you have put in, without having to pay
anything back because it is already yours. What God
says is that the same free access to the credit that He
gave to Abraham, He has given to all of us. It is a credit
that is stored up based on your level of faith.

Strong faith means naming the thing you want and
then patiently waiting until the time comes to receive it.
It is knowing that you have it stored up for you and then
waiting for the God-appointed time to withdraw it.
Strong faith gets you on the receiving end. This is what
Abraham did. He waited in faith over the years to receive
what he had been promised.

Glorifying God

When you express the type of strong faith we discussed previously, it glorifies God. Abraham was blessed to receive the promise of the Lord in his old age.

And when Abraham was ninety years old and nine, the Lord appeared to Abram, and said unto him, I am the Almighty God; walk before me, and be thou perfect.

And I will make my covenant between me and thee, and will multiply thee exceedingly.

And Abram fell on his face: and God talked with him, saying,

As for me, behold, my covenant is with thee, and thou shalt be a father of many nations.

Neither shall thy name any more be called Abram, but thy name shall be Abraham; for a father of many nations have I made thee.
(Genesis 17:1-5)

Before Abram became Abraham, God made a promise to him. The promise didn't come through a prophet or an angel. It came directly to Abraham from God. So many people wait for the promise of God to come through a preacher or for the revelation of God to come through a visiting prophet or someone on television. But

God says you can ask Him yourself about His promises if you go directly to Him. Genesis 17:3 says that Abram fell to his face, and God—not an angel, not a pastor, nor a prophet, but God—talked with him.

Do you really want to have strong faith? Stop depending on other sources. Get into the Word of God. That is how you will develop strong faith and glorify God. It will not come through some emotional display. It will not come because you attend a church service or because you watch a particular television program. Strong faith will come when you get into a place where you can hear directly from God.

God spoke to Abraham and told him He was going to bless them with a child, even though their biological clocks said they could not produce one. You may think the time has already passed for God to do something in your life. You may feel you will never go back to school and get a good education. You may feel you will never pursue your goals and dreams because you are too old. You say all of these negative things and more. *But who gave you the authority to pronounce death over your life?*

Abraham's first thought was that it was impossible for them to have children since he was 99 years old. When Sarah was given the word, she couldn't believe it at first either. She thought it wasn't possible. But God made a promise. And Abraham believed it despite the overwhelming evidence that it could never happen. Strong faith has to do with what God has said. If He said it, you should wait for it even though much time has passed. God's Word *cannot* return to Him void. Believe in what God said and wait for the promise to manifest itself.

The Bible says Abraham believed God and didn't waiver. Strong faith has to do with holding onto the promise no matter what. Believe in what God has said no matter what the obstacles around you may be. If you believe it because God said it, it will come to pass in your lifetime.

No doubt, as years went by, Abraham and Sarah thought they had no chance of seeing it fulfilled in the normal way. They were in the advanced stages of life. It would have been easier for them to trust God for a child when they knew that it would have been humanly possible. But what happens when you get to the place where it's not humanly possible? That place is one of pure faith where God wants you to trust Him alone.

For 15 years I believed that God would give us children, even though doubt sometimes entered. People would say to us that maybe the Lord didn't want us to have kids. If I didn't have enough faith, I might have thought it was not the will of the Lord for us to have children. But I knew what God promised me. I didn't swallow what everyone said. They said I had missed it this time and should have adopted children. I had thought of this possibility myself. But each time God reminded me of His promise. The most amazing thing is that God fulfilled His promise at a time when we least expected it. We tried and tried to have a child only to become frustrated. Finally we got to the place where we said, "It's not by our might but by Your power and Your Spirit that this will happen." We finally let go and let God. That's when God stepped in and my wife became pregnant with our son.

When you stagger not at the promise of God, faith will come alive, and He will do what He said He would do in your life. When the news first comes of your dream being fulfilled, you will not know what to do. You will be so amazed and thankful!

The Essentials of Faith

In this chapter we have been discussing strong faith. Let me share with you three essential characteristics of strong faith that will bring you into an experience of all that God has for you in this realm.

1. **Strong faith must have a valid content.** Valid content involves a revelation from God. What is the valid content in your life? *Have you heard what God has said?* Did God promise you something? You must have a valid revelation from God. You will never have a strong faith if you have no revelation. You must have something to hold onto; if not, you will stagger or waver. But when you have a revelation, you will know beyond a shadow of a doubt the awesome power of God.

2. **Strong faith must have a valid object.** That valid object must be God. God is the giver of revelation. It is

impossible to have faith without Him. All you will have are broken promises. *The object of your faith is God who is the Creator.* He is the one who reveals what He is going to give to you. Faith happens in this sequence: I believe God, I know He said He would do it, and now I believe Him for it.

3. **Strong faith is not hope and yet it rests upon it.** Faith is in the present tense. Faith is the substance of things hoped for, the evidence of things not seen. Hope is future tense. Faith and hope are two different things. However, faith works with hope to bring about all that God has promised you.

When you develop strong faith in God, He will be glorified and you will see His promises fulfilled in Your life beyond your expectations!

God does not call everyone in the crowd.
If you know how
to get His attention, God will call *you*
out of the crowd. Before you know it,
people will wonder how it is
that you were beside them one day
and the next day you are
far ahead of them. You can tell them the
reason is because you were
responding to God's call.

Don't Quit Your Faith

And they came to Jericho: and as he went out of Jericho with his disciples and a great number of people, blind Bartimaeus, the son of Timaeus, sat by the highway side begging.

And when he heard that it was Jesus of Nazareth, he began to cry out, and say, Jesus, thou son of David, have mercy on me,

And many charged him that he should hold his

peace: but he cried the more a great deal, Thou, son of David, have mercy on me.

And Jesus stood still, and commanded him to be called. And they called the blind man, saying unto him, Be of good comfort, rise; he calleth thee.

And he, casting away his garment, rose, and came to Jesus.

And Jesus answered and said unto him, What wilt thou that I should do unto thee? The blind man said unto him, Lord, that I might receive my sight.

And Jesus said unto him. Go thy way; thy faith hath made thee whole. And immediately he received his sight, and followed Jesus in the way. (Mark 10: 46-52)

This story occurred in Jericho where we find a blind man named Bartimaeus. Bartimaeus heard of the miracles Jesus had performed and decided he was going to ask Jesus to heal him. When he arrived at the place where Jesus, his disciples, and a crowd of people were, Bartimaeus could not locate him because he was blind. Desperately he cried out to Him with a loud voice, "Thou son of David, have mercy on me!" The man couldn't see, but found Jesus anyway. If a blind man can get the attention of Jesus, what's stopping you?

It's strange how people can come to church, sit in the congregation and hear God, see the awesomeness of God, and still not be touched by Him. These people even wonder how visitors can come into the midst of the congregation and get so much more out of the service than they did.

It Is Your Destiny

When you're determined to see the glory of God in your life, don't allow anyone to stop you. If God sends you somewhere, don't allow people to keep you from going there and don't let their attitude prevent you from receiving the fullness of all that He has for you.

Don't let any person or thing stop your faith, your trust, and your confidence in the Lord. Don't let anyone stop you from being where God ordained you to be. The problem with the body of Christ is that we act as if we're trying to win a popularity poll. We want people to like us and don't want to offend them. If they stand between you and what God has for you, then go ahead regardless of what they may think. It's your destiny we're talking about.

You have to stick your chest out and declare that you are not in a popularity contest. "You may like me or you may not like me. But I won't let you stand between me and what God has for me." You can't trifle with your salvation. You can't trifle with your destiny.

Unfortunately, some people will never go anywhere in life because they are too concerned about what people think. Bartimaeus didn't care that the crowd rebuked him and tried to prevent him from shouting to Jesus. He just shouted all the more.

You don't have to fear other people and what they say about you! The more people talk about you, the more you should talk to the Lord. The more people try to block you, the closer you should draw to the Lord! When the enemy tries to tempt you to quit your faith, you should tell the devil you have come too far to turn back now. If you're going to cross the goal line, you can't listen to the devil. Tell yourself you see the goal post and your destiny is on the line.

Football players can't afford to be wimps on the field. In all the years that I've watched football, I've never seen a player approach another player in a halfhearted manner. They charge at each other with heavy pads on their shoulders which says they mean business and are determined to cross the goal line. That's how it has to be with your Christian walk. You have to reach your God-given goals. You can't let anything or anyone stop you. You shouldn't care how big the enemy looks. If God be for you who can be against you? (Rom. 8:31)

Bartimaeus didn't quit when the crowd tried to rebuke him. The Bible says he shouted and shouted, "Thou son of David, have mercy on me." Jesus stopped and said, "Call him." Out of all the people that were around, Jesus stopped and called one man. God does not call everyone in the crowd. If you know how to get God's attention, God will call you out of the crowd. Before you know it, people will wonder how it is that you were beside them one day and the next day you are far ahead of them. You can tell them the reason is because you were responding to God's call.

What Would You Have Him Do?

Jesus asked Bartimaeus what he would like Him to do. With all the people standing around, Jesus asked one person what he wanted. Today, God is asking you, "What will you have me do for you? Will you continue to believe in Me or are you going to quit your faith?" Will you respond by saying you are discouraged and ready to give up? Being discouraged is one of the top reasons for people not reaching their destiny. They are discouraged because either they have not heard from the Lord or are impatient because what He has said has not yet come to pass.

I spoke to a pastor recently who said, "Bishop, I need counseling because my church is not growing." He told me he was frustrated and felt he was at a crossroads in his ministry. He wanted to know if he should close up the church and embark on another career. I asked him how long his church had been in existence, and his response to me was "Two months." Many of us want to laugh at that preacher, but if you were in the same position, you might have quit after only one week.

Even though God has spoken to you several times about many things, you may be tempted to quit believing because you let people come between you and your God. If so, you must realize that people are influencing you more than God and take steps to change the situation.

Building Perseverance

The working of your faith builds *perseverance*. It matures you in your faith. *If you have not been through any difficulties, you have not been tested.* You may be tempted to make hasty decisions about your job because you are coming up against some challenges there. You have to align everything you do with the Word of the Lord. Sometimes you can miss your destiny because you are too hasty. Prematurely quitting your job will make you miss your destiny.

I can speak from my own experience. I have had many struggles in life even though I have been faithful to God. I did not quit, however. Through all of my struggles, I stayed close to the Lord. I sowed into the Lord's work throughout the difficulties. God saw fit to bless me with material things and, most importantly, with a growing ministry.

God has brought you from afar. I am sure that some people have tried to stand in your way. But you must not quit. It's fighting time now. Defend who you are! Stand firm in your faith and tell them you're not backing down because you have come too far to quit.

I will receive what I desire because I will confess it with my mouth, believe it in my heart, and then I shall receive it. You can't let people stop you. When you attend church, you can't let people stop you from pressing into God. The enemy may plant people in the congregation to stop you. Everyone who attends church is not saved. The enemy will plant people in the congregation to deter you from fulfilling your purpose in God. They may be used by the devil and not even realize it. I have seen people leave the church and quit their faith over trivial matters. Do not quit your faith! I have seen people make stupid mistakes and become confused. According to them, one minute the Lord said this, the next minute the Lord said that. But the Lord is not the author of confusion. His Word will help you determine what He is saying to you.

A few years ago, I received two telephone calls the very same day. One was from Atlanta, Georgia, and the other was from overseas. Both calls offered me a "bigger and better" church. They offered more money, housing, and transportation. During this time, it seemed as though all hell was breaking loose at The Faith Center. Now you can guess what I was thinking. I was ready to leave The Faith Center. The offers were tempting, but I didn't quit because God did not tell me to quit. I kept my faith in the vision He had given me.

Then the Lord spoke to me clearly and said, "Son, I placed you here to build character in you." He reminded me what had happened years before when I had a job in the North Broward Hospital District. They were not paying me enough money, and I was about to quit. So, I interviewed for a job at Eastern Airlines. They were going to pay me three times what the hospital was paying, plus I would have the opportunity to travel the world free. Here I was in a dead end job and Eastern Airlines looked like a window of opportunity.

The following day I went to work at the hospital, fully prepared to give my resignation and one week notice in order to start the job at Eastern. Then the Holy Spirit spoke clearly to me and said that not all that looks like gold is gold. He told me not to quit my job. When He said that, I knew it was God. Less than two weeks later, Eastern Airlines went bankrupt! I remained at the hospital for over nine years. When I left, I was earning good money, but I could have lost it all because of greed. But instead, I listened to God and followed His guidance.

Standing Your Ground

When I look at my own life, there have been times when I felt in my heart that the challenges and pressures were just too much. At times they seemed unbearable. Handling the bills and learning how to properly structure the ministry was almost too much to deal with. People sometimes didn't cooperate. As soon as I fixed one department, another department was in need of repair. When I got that department fixed, the first department had problems again.

So, I asked God what I needed to do. At the time, we

were in the middle of a construction project at the convention center. I told God I was tired and frustrated and felt people didn't care. The enemy will make you think people don't care and everybody is against you, but that isn't true. In reality, there are always more people who are for you than there are against you.

We began the convention center project with a budget of more than $200,000 and it ended up costing more than $400,000 to complete the building. Right about that time, I attended a conference. At the end of one session, the offering was about to be taken. Bishop Carlton Pearson challenged the audience to sow a percentage of what we needed God to give us. For example, if we believed God for $500,000, he asked us if we would sow $500. I can tell you that I had $480 in my pocket. I told the Lord this was money my wife and I needed to use on the trip. Then God reminded me I had my credit card, so we would still be fine. The Lord spoke to me and said, "Obey." I took out the $480 reluctantly and sowed it. I wrote on the offering envelope, "Lord, we need the money. Father, I am sowing the $480 because we need about $280,000 to complete the building and I don't know where the rest of the money will come from."

I left the envelope on the offering table and walked away in faith. The next week the contractors needed their money and I still didn't know where it would come from. Then I got a telephone call from someone who asked me if I needed some money and how much did I want. I tried to be nice and told him that $50,000 would be good. He repeated his question again, saying he was asking for the last time. "How much money do you want?" I told him that I needed about $280,000. The caller said it was a done deal! I gave $480 in the offering at the conference and didn't stop believing God to supply what we needed. I stood my ground.

How much are you *losing* because you quit believing God to meet your needs? I'm not just talking about money; I'm talking about every area of your life. *Don't miss your destiny because you're ready to throw in the towel.*

The Apostle Paul said, "Finally, my brothers, be strong in the Lord and in the power of his might" (Eph. 6:10). Don't quit your faith. Hold on to what God has said to you. You have to *stand* on the Word of God and *believe* it and *wait* for its fulfillment. Then you will see Him move mightily on your behalf!

Your love for God shouldn't be based
on what you can get from Him.
When you're mature, you can go to God and
not have to ask Him for a blessing.
What you will ask for is a heart
to serve Him and worship Him.
You won't have to ask Him to pay off your
credit cards or to make you debt free.
You'll be mature enough to realize this will
happen when you seek Him first.

Perseverance Takes You
to Maturity

My brethren, count it all joy when ye fall into divers temptations;

Knowing this that the trying of your faith worketh patience.

But let patience have her perfect work, that ye may be perfect and entire, wanting nothing.
James 1:2-4

James opens his letter by describing the various testing that all of us as believers are going to encounter. He didn't promise the believer a life filled with happiness. In fact, he told us in verse two to count our trials as pure joy. When you count something, you give value to it. "Count it all joy" means to value it with joy when you find yourself in these temptations. Although contrary to our human nature, it's an attitude that will truly transform our lives.

All of your negative experiences should be accepted with great joy. I know it's hard for you and I to meet the challenges of life and the temptations we face on a daily basis. The tests of life are difficult. If we are honest, we must admit we don't really want to go through them. Those are the most difficult times of your life. All of us would like to live happily ever after, go to work without any problems, and receive a raise every week. It would be nice not to ever have problems with your husband or wife. It would be nice if your mortgage payments were paid up a year in advance. It would be nice if your car never broke down.

Let me bring you back to reality. None of this will ever happen. You and I will have to face the challenges of life. But according to James, these are the things in life we ought to accept with great joy.

The Acceptance Attitude

How can you accept challenges with great joy? You must take on a different attitude that says, "Well, bless God. My faith is being tested." You must count it all joy for example, when you are not experiencing health, or when you have financial troubles. How can you? You have to believe what it says in the book of James. All trials and testings are there to help you have faith in God and bring you to a higher level of spiritual maturity.

You'll never become mature in Christ if you're not tested. It's the testing of your faith and the trials you and I go through that develop character in us and increase our trust in the Lord. You must come to the place where you don't lean on your own understanding (Prov. 3:5). You may not be able to make sense out of anything that's happening around you, but you *can* consider it all joy.

For example, if on Tuesday your car gets wrecked, on Wednesday you have a fight with your spouse, on Thursday your kids have their bikes stolen, on Friday the boss lays you off, on Saturday you go to the grocery store and the prices have gone way up, and on Sunday you go to church only to discover that your church has moved without telling you—that is real bad! Now I'm *not* saying that you should ask God to give you more trouble. What I *am* saying is that in your spirit you should count it all joy. You should thank God because you know He is teaching you something. There is a lesson to learn in the midst of your difficulties.

God can accomplish much positive work in you through testing. Your eyes may not see it, and you may not fully comprehend it at the time. But when it's over, others will also benefit from hearing about what you have learned and how you made it through the test. That will build their faith to assure them that God will make a way somehow for them, too.

Patience and perseverance will lead you to a higher level of maturity. You can tell when Christians are mature—they will not be shaken, even when the ground all around them is sinking. A mature Christian is able to stand and trust the Lord when things around them are falling apart.

Testing of Your Faith

Consider it joy when you fall into or you are faced with trials of many kinds, because you know that the testing of your faith develops perseverance.

When James says, "the testing of your faith," it's not you, but your faith that's being tested. It's testing *what* you believe. It's testing *whom* you believe in. It's testing the very *foundation of what you stand on.* James wrote it very clearly. He said when you are faced with trials, you should know it's the testing of *your faith* and not the testing of *you,* the person.

What you are up against are the forces of darkness that want to contradict your faith. You say you believe in God. You say you know God will make a way. But the devil wants to come against your faith. It's not about you. Do you really believe the devil wants to come against you? He has better sense than that. The devil knows he can't pick on anyone in the body of Christ.

Remember the story of Job? The devil knew he could not walk into Job's life and bother him without permission from God. Everything you're going through right now, God gave the devil permission to do. When God and Satan had a conversation about Job, the devil said, "Consider your servant Job." The devil said that Job would curse God if he were placed into the devil's hands. So, God told the devil to go ahead and test him. God knew He had a hedge of protection around his soul. But the devil thought he could turn him away from God. Job may have been weak in his flesh, *but it was God working in Job that could not be reckoned with.*

Your flesh cannot fight the devil; he will win every time. But when he comes up against the One who is living inside of you, the Bible says, "Greater is he that is in you than he that is in the world" (1 Jo. 4:4).

Patience Is a Process

The second part of James 1:2 states that "perseverance develops patience." Testing takes you through a process. Through that process you develop trust in the

Lord. You learn to wait on the Lord and be faithful and consistent in all you do. The testing of your faith develops something in you that the devil doesn't like. When you develop patience and perseverance, you decide you don't care what the devil does to you—just as when Job said, "Though He slay me yet will I trust Him" (Job 13:15). The devil didn't know he was teaching Job to be firm. Whatever you are going through, you *can* go through it! Job went through it. He had an opportunity to bail out. He could have cursed God and died. He lost his wealth, his kids, and his health. But in the end, the devil was actually helping Job become the person that God wanted him to be. Then Job gained everything back and much more!

Perseverance must finish its work so you may be mature and complete, not lacking anything. In order for the glory and power of God to be poured into your life, in order for you to get to the place of having more than just enough, you have to learn to be patient. You must also be willing to endure the entire test. The testing of your faith works perseverance in you and takes you to a level where you are mature in God and lack nothing.

The trials you and I face today are doing a work in us, developing our patience and perseverance to finish the work God began. We love to start things, but we don't like to finish things. We've started projects at home, on the job, with our finances and relationships, and not completed them.

A few years ago, I visited a neighborhood that had

beautiful landscaping around the homes. I really fell in love with it. That afternoon, I kept picturing the landscaping and comparing it to my own. I decided that mine needed improvement, so I was going to change it that day. I must say I started the work out of ignorance and not with good planning. I hadn't first determined the cost involved. I hadn't considered the tools needed to complete the job. I hadn't considered the manpower needed to complete it. Nevertheless, with all of these things against me, I began the project.

I went to the store and spent a lot of time determining what I needed, such as potted plants, a wooden fence, and other things. I wanted my landscaping to look just like the ones I had seen that morning.

I returned home well after 3:00 P.M. full of energy. I soon realized I had more work to do than I expected. It was necessary to cut away old hedges and chop down some trees. That didn't stop me. The hours continued to pass as I chopped and sawed, and dug and cut until I had water blisters all over my hands. But I didn't stop.

By 8:00 P.M. I was ready to plant. I started to place them around the area I had prepared. It was not until I stood back and took a good look that I realized I had only completed one side of the yard. It was well after 9:00 P.M. by then, and I still had another side of the yard to start and complete. That's when I really started to feel the pain. Well, I quit. I took the topsoil, the gravel, the little stones, and put them in my garage. I took the tools and put them away, too. I ended up selling the house without finishing the other side of the garden and gave the materials to the new owners so they could finish it.

What's the point? The Bible says that perseverance must *finish its work* so that you may be mature, lacking nothing. What was the mistake that I made? First of all, I didn't sit down in the beginning to determine what it would take to get from point A to point B. What tools did I need? How much time would be involved in completing this task? I got excited and thought that at least starting the project was better than doing nothing at all. But starting the work and not finishing it can be just as bad as not starting it in the first place!

Many of us are placed in a position where we don't want to have patience. We need to say, "God, give me patience so that I'll know the right thing to do." Patience will teach you to complete what you start. It will enable you to have the career you always wanted. It will get you the degree you never earned. Patience will work in you until you have the perseverance to finish the task.

Many Christians start out at Calvary, confessing their sins to Him, but not growing in their faith. Now some of you are still at Calvary. Nowhere in the Bible does God say He wants you to stay at Calvary. He wants you to move and grow! Even Jesus left Calvary. He didn't stay on the cross.

Irritations that used to bother you five years ago shouldn't bother you today. Five years from now, you shouldn't expect to be the same Christian you are today.

Why? Because you should have grown in the Lord over time.

You must understand that God's time clock is not your time clock. So, you must be patient and believe God while perseverance finishes its work in you. Perseverance means you keep believing and moving on no matter what happens. It's not standing still and confessing, "God I know You will make a way, I believe what the Bible says, I know my faith is strong in the Lord." Those are good words, but perseverance also involves action, putting your confession into practice—keeping on when the going gets tough.

Knowing, Believing and Acting

Perseverance is all about *knowing* and *believing* that God will make a way and *acting* on it. It is about *saying,* "God I don't see the way out, but I know You will make a way. God, I don't understand it, it's confusing to me, but God, I trust you anyway and I am going to finish the work. I believe that You began a good work in me and are able to perform it until the day of Jesus Christ (Phil. 1:6).

"Father, I know you are going to finish the course You started in me. My family will not laugh at me, my coworkers will not laugh at me, my enemies will not laugh at me because I will finish the work. Whatever You began in me, I will finish because I am willing to allow patience to develop within me. I am willing to become mature."

Do you know why many Christians today cannot testify and encourage other people? Nothing positive ever comes from their mouth because they have never been through anything and finished the test! As soon as they begin to go through a difficulty, they cry to God to deliver them from it. They think they will die. Because they don't wait on the Lord, they have no testimony. They don't allow the Lord to teach them anything. But when you have walked through difficult testings yourself and someone comes to you and says they can't go on, you can tell them you know God will make a way because He did it for you.

Finish the Course

The Apostle Paul said he fought the good fight; he kept the faith; he finished his course (2 Tim. 4:7). Do you want God to finish the work He started in you? If you desire to marry, you ought to have patience. Let that patience finish the work in you. Be anxious for nothing. Don't tell yourself you're too old. Don't be pressured by society and rush into it. You must give God time to work. You must learn to be patient with what He is doing. Don't ever try to rush things before their time. God may show you the right spouse, but that doesn't necessarily mean the time is right for marriage. Before you try to take what God has promised you, be patient and let Him finish the work both in the other person and in you. When the time comes for you to receive your promise, you will be able to handle it properly.

It's very important to wait on God patiently for the desires of life. If you select a husband or wife before God has completed the work within both of you, serious problems could develop. If God doesn't finish His work, you will end up marrying someone who cannot truly love you because they're still in the development stage.

Lacking in Nothing

Let perseverance and patience finish their work in you. Before you get excited, allow God to finish the work in you so that you will be complete. Patience brings you to a level of maturity so that you will learn to wait on God. You need to get to the place where you are lacking nothing. You need to get to the place where if someone does not give you what he or she promised, you are still complete because you are not lacking anything. You need to get to the place where you are still complete even if the promise is not fulfilled. The promise you were going to receive really does not come from another person anyway, it comes from the One who made the person.

In whom are you going to trust? Are you going to trust in the Lord? When you have patience, you learn to trust in God and no one else. Your boss may refuse to give you that promotion. Maybe God is trying to say that if you'll be patient, He can move upon your boss to give you a raise. If he tries to block it, God may even remove him or provide you with a new job at the proper time.

Perseverance brings you to a level where you depend on God instead of people. Then you will understand that you are complete and lack nothing in Him. You don't worry about material things anymore. The car and the house and the money mean nothing. Now it takes a lot to get to that point, but perseverance will bring you there.

A report was published recently that said Christians are more attracted to sermons about wealth than anything else. Millions of books, videos, and tapes are sold about wealth. You just say, "wealth," and they claim it. *Is that all there is to God?* You should eventually get to the place where you don't need to seek God for a new car or a new house. Do not seek God just because you want Him to work some sort of miracle in your life. You should be mature enough to want to seek God because He is good and you want to be around Him. He doesn't have to give you anything else in this world to make you happy. *You seek Him because you love Him.*

Your love for God shouldn't be based on what you can get from Him. When you're mature, you can go to God and not have to ask Him for a blessing. What you will ask for is a heart to serve Him and worship Him. You won't have to ask Him to pay off your credit cards or to make you debt free. You'll be mature enough to realize this will happen when you seek Him first. *What you should want is more of Him.*

When you seek Him alone, you'll start to rearrange your life. You won't pray for things. You'll walk into your house and thank God for all His blessings. You'll remember when you did not have a house and you'll thank him for everything He has already given you. You'll thank him for your job. You'll learn to bless the Lord at all times. His praise will continue to be in your mouth. You'll bless Him even when things do not look good. You'll praise Him anyway.

When you reach that level of maturity, your attitude and your worship will change. I pray to God today that you will allow patience and perseverance to mature you. I pray that you will learn to walk through your difficulties with joy. *When you are mature you will tell God you want Him because of who He is, not because of what He can give you!*

About the Author

Bishop Henry B. Fernandez answered the call of God to reach the world for Christ in 1985 when he moved from Brooklyn, New York to Fort Lauderdale, Florida. He became an ordained minister in 1988 and founded The Faith Center (formerly known as Plantation Worship Center) in 1991 with his wife, Dr. Carole Fernandez. Within a short period of time, the ministry experienced monumental growth and now has a membership of more than 5000.

His professional career began in the travel industry where he developed business and financial acumen that he now uses to help build the Kingdom of God. He is a sought after motivational/financial planning speaker who shares practical steps toward debt-free living. As CEO of the Plantation Economic Development Corporation, he has helped establish several businesses including a beauty center, fitness center, convention center, bookstore, printing company, and restaurant.

Bishop Fernandez holds quarterly homebuyer's seminars in order to equip people with the necessary knowledge required to purchase a home. He is a visionary who is committed to helping everyone prosper in the natural as well as the spiritual realm. This commitment is demonstrated in his establishment of the University of Fort Lauderdale which has been fully accredited by the Florida State Board of Independent Colleges and Universities since May 1996. Degrees at the Bachelors, Masters and Doctorate levels are offered. He also established the Henry B. Fernandez Institute for Learning to offer biblical courses to ministers and lay leaders who desire a solid foundation in understanding God's Word.

Bishop Fernandez is overseer to the Jamaica Worship Center in Kingston, the Montego Bay Worship Center in Montego Bay, Jamaica and The Faith Center West in Phoenix, Arizona. He is a pastor to many pastors in a network of churches that he has established.

For more information about Bishop Fernandez or to book speaking engagements, write to:

Henry Fernandez Ministries
P.O. Box 9726
Ft. Lauderdale, FL 33310

Also by Henry Fernandez

Divine Love
Henry Fernandez shares practical ways to express the divine love that God has placed in our hearts. It's the kind of love that counts when human love isn't enough. *Divine Love* is a great book for individuals, couples, and for family or small group Bible studies.
ISBN 1-58169-006-1   64 pg. PB $6.95

Other books from Evergreen Press

The Power of Forgiving Robert Strand
In an easy-to-read style, Robert Strand presents true stories of exceptional forgiveness along with practical insights from the Scriptures.
ISBN 1-58169-050-9 96 p. PB $5.95

The Power of Thanksgiving Robert Strand
Stories and teaching that demonstrate the difference that a lifestyle of thanksgiving can make in our lives.
ISBN 1-58169-054-1 96 p. PB $5.95

The Power of Gift Giving Robert Strand
Through numerous short stories, Scripture, and teaching, Robert Strand demonstrates how gifts can be effective, how giving can change lives, and how your gift can be all-important.
ISBN 1-58169-055-X 96 p. PB $5.95

Life Is A Gold Mine Dr. John Stanko
This book teaches you how to effectively and efficiently fulfill your life's mission. It shows you how to set goals, organize, and manage your time wisely.
ISBN 1-58169-059-2 208 p. PB $11.95

The Paradigm Quest (fiction) Jean Koberlein
An allegory written in the style of Hind's Feet on High Places, it challenges you to reach higher and go further to find fresh vision and purpose and embark on your own search.
ISBN 1-58169-052-5 176 p. PB $10.95

A Gathering of Eagles Col. Jimmie Dean Coy
More than 300 Medal of Honor recipients, ex-POWs, and military, political, and religious leaders share their core beliefs about leadership, success, and significance.
ISBN 1-58169-049-5 320 p. PB $14.95

The Little Book of Business Wisdom Brian Banashak

Business wisdom for the novice and veteran alike. Packed with 88 principles for success—each with Scripture verse and testimony.
ISBN 1-58169-041-X 96 p. PB $5.95

Proverbs of Success John Grogan

The heart and soul of highly effective people. John Grogan has been a professional trainer and speaker for more than 30 years. This book captures the essence of the wisdom he has shared with audiences around the globe.
ISBN 1-58169-045-2 96 p. PB $5.95

Be Encouraged Leona Dorsey

A ministry of poetic messages for today's urban women to uplift your mind, body, and spirit.
ISBN 1-56043-248-9 80 p. PB $8.95

How to Memorize the Books of the Bible John Lee Davis

If you've ever fumbled through the Word looking for verses, here's an easy way to memorize the names and sequence of the books of the Bible.
ISBN 1-58169-039-8 32 p. Softcover $4.95

Available from your local bookstore, Amazon.com,
BN.com or call 888-670-7463